A Saint's Last Tear

By

Brad Roe

ISBN: 1-4140-3499-7 (e-book)
ISBN: 1-4140-3498-9 (Paperback)

Library of Congress Control Number: 2003098558

This book is printed on acid free paper.

Printed in the United States of America
Bloomington, IN

1stBooks - rev. 04/06/04

"The famous Symeon, the great wonder of the world, is known by all the subjects of the Roman Empire and has also been heard of by the Persians, the Medes, the Ethiopians; and the rapid spread of his fame as far as the nomadic Scythians has taught his love of labor and his philosophy. I myself, though having all men, so to speak, as witnesses of his contests that beggar description, am afraid that the narrative may seem to posterity to be a myth totally devoid of truth. For the facts surpass human nature, and men are wont to use nature to measure what is said; if anything is said that lies beyond the limits of nature, the account is judged to be false by those uninitiated in divine things. But since earth and sea are full of pious men educated in divine things and instructed in the grace of the all Holy Spirit, who will not disbelieve what is said but have complete faith in it, I shall make my narration with eagerness and confidence. I shall begin at the point at which he received his call from on high." (Theodoret of Cyrrhus 440 A.D.)

CHAPTER 1

I somehow became convinced that joining a gym would save me. I don't know how I came to that conclusion at such a young age, but I do know that it happened.

Yoga is sort of fun, in a self-mutilating, muscle-straining sort of way, but it certainly doesn't save people, in the religious sense. Neither does practicing Yoga in strange places with other strange and estranged men. It does do wonders for the breathing though. I breathe better than most people, but that's not all that exciting either. Most people breathe pretty well without spending thousands of dollars learning how.

It was three o'clock in the morning and I had just eaten my way out of a minor depression. I watched a thirty-minute infomercial filled with beautiful people and good music. Most people on the show wore leotards of some sort. I began to feel inadequate and overweight all at once. I called the 800 number on the screen and paid for a year's membership to Pure USA Gym on State Street in Santa Barbara.

It took me a week of fretting before I actually made my way down to the gym for my initial meeting with an official trainer. I chose a Friday when I knew my boss Peter would be spitting and shooting at beer cans in Tulsa for the weekend. When I got there, my life instantly changed. It took me almost a year to escape from that gym and the people I met there. It was a year I will never forget, emotionally or financially. That's what you get for being an insomniac, or at least for believing in people.

The gym had an eerie feeling to it. There was too much effort spent on the atmosphere and the people at the front desk seemed too happy to be making seven dollars an hour. Maybe they were on go-go pills. There were prints on the wall with words like 'Teamwork" and a picture of dolphins swimming together, or "Strength" and a picture of a grizzly bear tearing the head off a salmon swimming upstream.

I stopped to get a drink of water and out of the corner of my eye I spotted Alan, the Vodka Thief, from college. I hadn't seen him in over two years, not since the catering catastrophe with the Russian diplomats.

"Simeon," he yelled, "I can't believe you're here."

"Hey Alan," I said. "It's been a long time"

"Yeah, it has. How are things going?"

"Okay, I guess. I'm writing for a tractor magazine in town and taking classes in Ancient Greek at night, and I thought I would come and take a look at the gym."

I didn't tell him I had joined at 4:00 in the morning, shaking with pangs of guilt after having polished off 14 pieces of pizza during the night, and that I needed to get in shape.

"Well," Alan said, "welcome, to PURE USA GYM. I have made my home here and I would be honored to introduce you to B.D. and the rest of the gang."

"Thanks," I said.

"Our Yes To Yoga class is starting in four minutes so come over and say hello to B.D."

"Yes To Yoga?" I thought to myself. Maybe that's what I need. I think I will skip my meeting with the trainer and take that class with Alan. I had on sweatpants that afforded me plenty of stretching room. It was decided.

We walked over and, for an instant, I wondered if Alan still had that bottle of vodka hidden in the trunk of his car and if his parents had gotten any better at loving him. Then he introduced me to B.D. It was like getting run over by a John Deere tractor driven full throttle by a roaring drunk farmer. After six months of describing tractors and farmers and managing to make both sound interesting, it baffles me why this next moment, which lasted a year, is so hard for me to put into words. So many things happened, my life went in so many different directions, that when I think about him and what he did to me, I get confused.

3

B.D. reminded me of one of the gladiators from that old Kirk Douglas movie, *Spartacus*. He was short, tanned and muscular. He smelled like he had just showered with a revolutionary soap/shampoo/body scrub and conditioner product. He smiled with beautiful, perfect white teeth and looked me right in the eyes with so much hope I almost fell down and kissed his feet. He exuded self-confidence and a belief in himself, and it seemed like he believed in me. He was the dad I never had, the dad Alan wanted, and I liked him. And, while I was shaking his small but firm hand, I couldn't help but think to myself that I had only come here to meet a trainer named Tiny. But that thought disappeared as I fell under the spell of B.D.

Alan made the introductions.

"Simeon, this is B.D., our leader."

"B.D. this is Simeon, a TSP."

I said, nervously, "I'm not sure what a TSP is, but it's very nice to meet you. I'm looking forward to taking the Yes For Yoga class with you."

He laughed. "That's Yes To Yoga. A TSP is a tall, sensitive person. I am glad you are here, Simeon, and since you're a friend of Alan's, why don't you join us this evening after class at the meeting place? Alan will give you directions."

"Great!" I exclaimed.

"I have to warm up, but we can talk more tonight," B.D. said and turned and walked away.

We spent the next hour in a heated room breathing through our noses and putting our bodies in uncomfortable positions. But I felt clean, tired and proud of myself. B.D. had paid special attention to me during the class, telling me I was doing well or saying, "Say Yes To Yoga, Simeon" and other encouragements. It made me feel good. I went home to change, and, for the heck of it, decided to go to the meeting place to find out what the whole thing was about. On my way to the shower I checked my message machine and it was Peter.

"Sim, it's Peter. I just drank eight warm beers, spit close to two cans of chewing tobacco onto the innocent ground and listened to five hours of discussion about a new tractor that picks up carrots, sorts them, peels them and then ships them directly to China. Hope you are well. See you in two days."

Alan had given me a flyer with the address of a coffee place in an alley in downtown Santa Barbara. It was called the Coffee Cat. I had never been there. I got dressed and drove down to meet them at 7:00 p.m. On the way there I started to feel uncomfortable, like my head was caving in, and my heart began to beat louder than usual. I was a little scared and confused. I didn't know exactly why I was driving there in the first place or what I was expecting to see. Who was this guy B.D. anyway? Was he a martial arts instructor? Herbologist? Yoga freak?

It didn't take me as long to find the meeting spot downtown as I thought it would. I didn't jump out of my car, however, once I found a place to park. I sat there stunned, thinking about all the people in China who ride their bikes around town. Do they all shower and change before going to their desks? Well, anyway, if I had it my way I would kill my television and only ride my bike. Just like the Chinese. It is a much better way to travel.

I got out of the car, thanked all the Chinese I had ever known for their courage in riding bicycles and headed into the Coffee Cat to meet Alan and B.D. I was grumpy, the kind of grumpy I feel when I have put myself into a situation that makes absolutely no sense. Here I was, just trying to get in shape after a bout with moderation, joining a gym and getting healthy. But I end up running into the Vodka Thief and getting myself roped into some meeting with a tanned man and who knows who else. I shouldn't have quit smoking. I should kill my car and buy a new bike.

The meeting place smelled like steamed milk mixed with patchouli oil. There was music playing just too loud. It was Wagner. Whenever I hear Wagner I think of a young girl being run down by German tanks in the Polish countryside.

"Hey, Simeon," said the Vodka Thief. "I was worried you weren't going to join us."

"Oh well, I thought I would come check it out."

"I'm glad you did, Simeon," said Alan.

"Anyway, get some green tea and come and sit down with the group. People are still making their way down here so we'll get started in a few minutes. And think about why you are here, because B.D. is going to ask you to introduce yourself and talk about some of the changes you're going to make in your life."

He turned his back and walked away wearing a stupid shirt. Changes? Why am I here? Introduce myself? This whole thing was going too far. I began to envy the Chinese, even with the monsoons. They don't have to introduce themselves to groups of strange people and talk about the changes they are going to make in their lives. They are too busy showering after the long bike ride from work. Lucky bastards.

I walked around the room, checking people out to make sure no one looked too odd, and took a seat somewhere in the back. I tried to laugh about the situation, but was startled when B.D. put his hand on my shoulder and squeezed it saying, "Come up front, Simeon, I want everyone to meet you."

I was more baffled than anything else. The fact that I actually stood up and followed the tanned one's orders confused me as well. As I stood up I noticed three men sitting in the corner of the room, uninvolved with our group. They were dressed up, and, by their smiles, I could tell they were genuinely proud to be sitting together. As I walked up to the front I heard one of them say, "I still think about the war." The other two nodded and agreed with their eyes. I don't know what war they were talking about, but I figured it was probably WW II. Maybe they fought together, maybe they saw death, destruction and liberation all in one day. Maybe they drank freshly liberated champagne in the cellar of a bombed-out French restaurant. Maybe they talked about their wives, the children they hadn't seen in years, things they were going to do when they first got home. Maybe they held a dying friend in their arms.

7

I turned my head from the three friends and I walked up to the front of the room. I wasn't nervous; I was a little flustered, however. I didn't really want to come to this stupid meeting in the first place, and now here I was, the keynote speaker.

"Everyone, this is our newest member, Simeon. Put your hands together with love, self-awareness and success," sang B.D.

"Now, Simeon, tell us why you are here," he said, looking at me.

I didn't want to talk, but something inside me pushed me ahead and thrust me into speaking to the group of drifters, needers and some confused, nice people.

"Hi, I'm Simeon. I'm a friend of Alan's and I'm here because B.D. invited me," I said.

"Tell us a little about yourself, Simey," prompted B.D.

No one has called me Simey since I was five years old. I don't know how B.D. found out about that name. It was a kind name, one that meant I was loved enough to have a nickname. Some people don't even get nicknames. Instantly, I felt like B.D. knew me, and I trusted him.

"Well, I am a writer, actually a journalist for a tractor magazine in town, and I am in my early twenties and am generally a kind person, with a few habits that tend to get in the way of me being a completely whole person, I suppose. I enjoy reading and thinking about God and people and I love children," I said.

"What habits get in your way, Simey?" B.D. asked.

"Well, I tend to think about food too often and I love cigarettes and cookies and chips and chocolate milk and beer and pizza and

Chinese food. And I know that I should be exercising more and that is why I joined Pure USA," I said.

Suddenly I started to feel dizzy and I realized I was standing up in front of a room full of people I didn't know, telling my life story. I began to get angry and wonder why it was that I always find myself in odd situations. It probably has something to do with the television. I made a mental note that the first thing I was going to do when I got home was, once and for all, kill my television. Note taken. I began, again, to envy the Chinese and their bikes. I just wanted to sit down, but B.D. asked me another question and when I looked at the group, everyone was smiling and seemed interested in what I was saying. So, I remained standing.

"Tell us about your smile, Simey. We have all noticed it, and we find it to be a light in the darkness, a jacket on a cold day, a blanket at night. We love your smile. Don't we?" B.D. asked the group. And the people stood up and began clapping, chanting, "Love, self-awareness, success, love, self-awareness, success." I liked it.

"My smile comes from within." My legs were rocking, subtly, back and forth. "It is there because I can look into my heart and see the good in life," I waxed. The clapping and chanting continued like a bass line.

"And I think that there are a few, maybe twenty, maybe a thousand, maybe five million in each generation of human beings that realizes the tightrope we are walking on."

Love, self-awareness, success.

9

"There is a group of people that feels in a very deep way the experience of life. These people tend to be artists, poets, writers and drug addicts. You see, the deep feelings and the self-awareness sometimes creates works of art and music and social commentary and fashion and voices, but it can also create depression, isolation, anxiety and death."

Love, self-awareness, success.

Then I started looking at everyone in the group. One at a time. And I slowed down, confidently.

"Thank you. Okay. Thanks."

I felt like the ruler of a small country. I wanted to put Sir or Duke in front of my name. The group continued to clap for longer than normal and I took my seat toward the back of the room next to the three old men telling their stories of war. I took a deep breath and felt, surprisingly, whole.

I waited in the back of the room for a minute as the people in the group stopped turning around in their chairs and smiling at me one at a time like dominoes, only backwards, and then B.D. stood up and said, "Thank you all for coming and meeting our newest member. As always, when we introduce someone new, that takes precedence over any other business. I am passing around a new catalog for Pure USA and I know that you will all want to pick up some new workout items. I designed all of them with the help of Elena, our Ecuadorian artist at the gym. Take them home and look them over and we will meet again next week and talk about the retreat weekend at the end of the month. And, Simeon, thank you for letting us know you, we would be honored to have you here next week and to see you at Pure USA. Good night, everyone." He walked through the crowd and out the door like a cat that knows something is outside.

I followed slowly, shaking hands with people and exchanging kind glances. I didn't feel like talking any more. I had told them my most intimate feelings, so idle talk seemed pointless. The Vodka Thief was talking to a beautiful girl handing out catalogs. That must be Elena, I thought. She looked at me for a second and then Alan followed her eyes toward my direction. I waved at him and walked to my car, hoping I wouldn't run into the tanned cat and hoping I would run into Elena.

CHAPTER 2

Peter returned from Tulsa and, in his usual testosterone-overload manner, would only talk about dreams, Sophia Loren and tropical resorts. I went along wholeheartedly. After the meeting with B.D. and the group and all, I didn't mind talking about nothing.

"I had this weird dream in Tulsa, man, after a night out with the cowboys," he said. "It was set in Reno, Nevada, which is strange because I've never been there. Anyway, I was on my way to star in a musical about animals that become human and change the world in three days, when my car suddenly stopped running. I remember being scared and wondering if someone was going to come into the car and hurt me. There was music playing in the background, almost like the soundtrack to a movie, and I kept looking in the rearview mirror. Then I saw my grandmother in the mirror, who's been dead for ten years. She was coming toward me in a wheelchair, dressed up in an evening gown and singing songs that my mom used to sing to me when I was a kid. It seemed like it took forever for her to reach the car. I just watched her and listened to all the music going on. I remember thinking that of all the people to come and help me in Reno, I wouldn't have chosen my grandmother. When she got close to the car I opened the door to greet her. She didn't respond and continued wheeling down the road. And then I woke up."

"Why didn't she stop?" I asked.

"Probably because she's dead," said Peter, with a nervous smile.

I think she didn't stop because she saw him dressed up like a Panda Bear on roller skates and was embarrassed the other people in heaven would see him and laugh at her. I didn't say that, of course. Peter turned his attention to his computer and we began work for the day. We had a deadline that afternoon and I was writing a story about Rod Hanward, a farmer in Kansas who fell in love with a tractor after he slept in the hollow engine cavity of an Allis-Chalmers. The tractor, according to Rod, had saved his life:

Rod is just a man. A farming man. A man who toils and labors every day no matter what the weather. He runs his family business, a farm outside of Salinas, with ten employees. Now, however, he has a new member on the team. An early model Allis-Chalmers sits on a platform atop his brand-new barn. To most of the townsfolk, stopping over at Rod's and looking at the Allis is the closest they will ever get to the Lincoln Memorial. It is just as solid, just as majestic and proud, and, to most, just as gut-wrenching. You see, Rod was out with the dogs last winter for a spot of hunting when the weather began to turn bad. He went looking for one of his wayward terriers when he slipped down a gully, seriously twisting his ankle and injuring his hip flexors. There he was, writhing in pain and unable to walk, with nothing to keep him company but the panting and barking of his faithful dogs. It began to get dark and cold. An hour passed, then another. The moon was trying to push its way through the storm clouds, but losing the nightly battle.

Rod began to panic. If the weather continued to get worse, it could be his last night on the farm. Out of the corner of his eye, he spotted the outline of a dark object. He hobbled over to the location of the object and felt around the perimeter. It was an abandoned tractor. Just like Rod, it was dirty, wet and alone. He struck a waterproof match he had found in his pocket and discovered the engine had been removed from the cavity and the cockpit was stripped. He found some branches and grass under the tractor that were still dry, put them in the cockpit, climbed into the engine cavity and made himself as comfortable as he could for the rest of the night. He was warm, protected from the elements and safe. An abandoned tractor saved Rod's life. The inscription on his barn below the monument reads:

Touched by an angel. An angel named Allis
Saved from the night, by a metal messenger
Toil as I may, I will never forget
The night I was saved by an angel named Allis
(Please put change or bills in the tray so I can keep the monument clean and safe for everyone, thanks, your man, Rod)

Peter thought the story was a bit melodramatic, but once I showed him the photos of thirty people in front of their cars staring up at Rod's monument to Allis, he went ahead and ran it, mostly unchanged.

That night, after work, I went back to Pure USA with the thought of working out, but more with the intention of looking at Elena one more time. Her eyes were amazing. I walked through the ever-steaming doors, up to the front desk manned (and womaned) by headset-wearing fitness freaks and asked to speak with Elena.

"May I tell her who wishes to speak with her?" the fat-free receptionist asked.

"Yeah, tell her it's Simeon."

"Great," said Miss Sweet and Low.

A few minutes later I heard Elena's singsong voice: "You must be Simeon, the new guy."

"I am," I said. "Thank you for seeing me."

"Are you interested in some new workout clothes?"

"I am, and I heard you designed them."

It was all I could get out. I had joined this gym because I felt guilty about not exercising, but right now I had no intention of perspiring. In fact, I was hungry and all I could think about was Chinese—not about their bikes and their showers this time, but about their food. It was then that I made the most fateful decision of my life: I decided to ask out Elena, who is short, with olive skin, rich black hair, huge eyes and a soothing voice that came from a culture rich with history and passion. I reacted just like any other stocky guy at the front desk of a strange gym would: my legs began to shake.

"What type of clothes are you interested in?" she asked in that angelic voice.

"All of them," I replied stupidly.

"Well," she smiled, realizing I was nervous, "why don't we start with the sweatshirts? I designed them all."

"Where were they manufactured?" I asked, just as stupidly as before.

"In China." She smiled.

"Beautiful country with lots of food and plenty of bikes." My answers were rapidly deteriorating into absolute babble.

15

"Yes, so I hear."

I was in love. Finally a girl who knows about all the bikes in China. It was all I could do to hold back my question about where they all shower. I'd get to that later. Maybe she would join me for dinner. Maybe she could eat with chopsticks. No forks for this couple. Oh, Elena, let me make you my wife, let me look into your eyes and find out about your grandmother and the stories she used to tell you about her village.

"Come in the back and you can try on some things."

In the back room she began to hold up different designs and put them on her chest as if she were wearing them. She glowed. How could she be so happy? Is that what happens to people who exercise? Do they all become so angelic and happy? If so, sign my ass up. I'm ready for the commitment because whatever I'm doing ain't working. She looked great in orange. And red. And light blue. The sweatshirt she was currently holding up read, "Pure USA Gym" on the front and on the back it said, "Time is money. Money is power. What time is it in your life?"

"Do you have anything a little more subtle?" I asked. She laughed. I made her laugh. Now all I had to do was make her hungry and ask her to dinner at The Chinese Kingdom down the street.

"How about this one?" she asked. It had "Pure USA Gym" on the front and "Say Yes To Yoga And Yoga Will Say Yes To You" on the back. I bought an orange one for $85, slipped it on and asked Elena the most important question of my life.

16

"You know, I was hungry when I came in here, in fact I still am, and there's this little place, actually it's a kingdom, but a small one, really, down the street and I..."

"Are you asking me to dinner?" she said.

"Well, yes, I am, in my own bumbling way."

"I'd love to, but let me check with B.D. to make sure he has someone to cover the office while I'm gone."

"Okay," I said to her as she left. I felt great. I pictured myself next to Julius Caesar marching into Rome at the head of our legions, having just vanquished the barbarian hordes. I wanted wine. I wanted my woman. I wanted a rubdown and a new outfit. I was in charge.

She came gliding back into the room. "I can go," she said.

"Now, right now?" I asked.

"Well, yes, I thought that's what you meant."

"Great, let me get my car and I'll pull up out front and pick you up."

My car. I suppose I should tell you about my car. It's a white 1970 Volvo two-door sedan. The interior is red, but not leather. The radio doesn't work, along with one of the windshield wipers (on the driver's side). It runs when it feels like it. I was talking to it now as I approached. "Please start, please fire up, white baby. If there was ever a time for you to help me out, it is now. Please, white prince, fire up." I got in, rubbed the dashboard with both hands and put the key in the ignition. I went through this ritual every time I got in the car. It was a crapshoot. Twenty-five percent of the time the car

17

would start fine, the rest of the time I would have to pump the gas and talk to the car for a few minutes before he finally turned over. I didn't want that to happen tonight.

But, of course, it did.

There I was, sitting in the parking lot of Pure USA, wearing an orange sweatshirt I had bought from the most beautiful girl in the world, who, in all her glory, was standing one hundred yards from me, waiting. Wondering. "What is he doing in the car? Why isn't it starting? Why am I having dinner with a guy in a thirty-year-old Volvo?" I began to sweat. I continued to rub the cracked, faded red dashboard over and over again. It wasn't working. It was time for drastic measures. I got out, popped the hood and went to Plan B. Sometimes if I unscrew the air filter and take it off, then get back in the car and pump the gas a few times, it will start. I did that. Now, my hands are dirty. Elena, the center of my universe, is pacing nervously. I take off the air filter, get back in the car, begin to pump over and over again and turn the key. Nothing but a faint, feeble whine. I panicked. By now, if I was Chinese, Elena and I would have ridden our bikes to dinner, showered somewhere, changed and we'd be sipping wonton soup with bits of crabmeat floating on top. I put my head in my hands, giving up, and I heard Elena's voice.

"Simeon, is the car okay?" she asked.

"I don't know what the problem is, it always fires right up," I replied.

"Why don't we leave the car here and walk to the restaurant? I don't mind the exercise," she offered. I was desperate and dejected. I couldn't even drive the most incredible woman in the world to dinner. I was at an all-time low. I planned on overeating when I got home. It was time for some changes in my life. I needed a car that worked. If I was going to make a place for Elena in my life, I had to upgrade my wheels. Maybe Peter would loan me some money or co-sign a loan. Who knows? I got up out of the car, smiled, realizing I was defeated, and decided to agree with her suggestion.

"I'm sorry, Elena, I'm embarrassed that my car won't start on our first date," I said, looking at the ground.

"Don't worry about it, Simeon. I think it's kind of funny."

"It is, I guess," I returned. "Well, let's walk and if we don't make it to the Chinese Kingdom we can eat somewhere else."

"Sounds good. Don't sweat the car thing. My car does that all the time," sang my sweet princess. Now I knew I was in love. What composure. What grace (maybe she had British relatives; I'd have to ask her later). Plus she has a bad car like mine. I was amazed at how much we had in common. I would love her forever, starting right now.

I walked next to her, always on the street side, in case a car decided to jump the curb, I would be the first to go and Elena would be saved. I also walked a little behind her so I could look at her perfect legs move in even more perfect rhythm. Her shoes were dirty—just a little bit, but enough to add character. Her hands looked soft and brown and moisturized. I was walking funny: bouncing, staring at her entire body, saving her from wayward automobiles and trying not to trip over my own feet and fall on my face, all at the same time. Tough job, but I was managing.

"So, Simeon, you're new at Pure USA, right?" she asked.

"Yes, I've only been a member a week."

"Have you been to one of the meetings?"

"Yeah, the other night at the Coffee Cat, downtown," I replied.

"Oh, that's right, you were the guy that talked about the poets and drug addicts and stuff. A lot of people were talking about your changes."

"Is that good or bad?" I asked.

"Good, I think," she said. "It takes a lot of courage to talk in front of B.D. and the other members."

"You know, Elena, I'm not really sure why I got up in front of the group in the first place. In fact, I'm not even sure what the group is or what it does. I just wanted to join a gym to get in better shape and I ran into an old friend from college who invited me to the meeting. What does the group do, anyway?" I asked. She smiled at me and kept walking, saying nothing. At least, not yet.

It's difficult for me to describe the next twenty minutes. I was nervous. I was happy. I was surprised. I was fearful. I was breathing heavily. Elena strode at quite a clip. I made a note to work on my walking in case I was thrust into this situation again. We made it all the way to the Chinese Kingdom and, as usual, there was a table available and everyone was smiling.

"Back again, huh?" said the shorthaired waitress as she grabbed two menus and began walking to the table.

"This one all right?" she asked.

"It's great," I said. "It's good to see you."

"Okay. All right. Thank you," she said, flustered, and walked away.

As we sat, I couldn't help but look out through the crowded kitchen door, searching for bikes resting on a wall or locked up against a pole. I spotted two old road bikes. I wondered if our waitress owned one of them and, if so, where was the shower? I would find it later. Elena got up from the table.

"I'll be right back, Simeon," she said. She seemed distant.

For some reason a picture of my dad popped into my head, though it was hardly the best time for that to happen. Maybe it was the Kingdom. I happen to know that one of the good things I inherited from him was a love of Chinese food. My mom told me that a few years ago. I began to wonder how he was doing and if he ever thought about me. He lives somewhere in Washington in a town with one of those strange Washington names and is an eye doctor. I hadn't seen him or talked to him in over twenty years. I think he would be proud of me, though—if he could see out of his little world for a few moments or remain conscious for more than a few hours at a time. I hope he would be proud. Elena was still in the bathroom.

"You want some more tea?" the waitress asked.

"Please."

I was beginning to wonder where Elena had gone. Maybe she had to wait in line for the restroom or something.

I began to eat those chip things they give you. I dipped one side of the chip in the red sauce and the other side in the yellow. Then I put the whole thing in my mouth.

I think what is most hurtful about my dad is that I don't think he cares where I am right now or what I'm doing. I wonder if he knows that I write for a tractor magazine or that I study Ancient Greek? I wish he did. But you want to know what I wish more? I wish that the image of my dad's weathered and slightly overweight face would disappear from the top of my hot tea so I could concentrate on lovely Elena, the Ecuadorian she-princess, ruler of all clothing at the gym. And so on.

I looked down at my tea and his face was still there. Just like when you stare at a full moon you can see the face of God. At least I used to be able to. I haven't tried in a while. Elena was still not back. I began to sweat. My stomach started hurting. My eyes were blinking at twice the normal rate. My palms were warm. Where is she? Maybe she's sick and doesn't want to tell me. Could she have locked herself in the restroom? Is she trapped? Should I go in there? I looked at my watch. Twenty minutes had passed. I waited a few more minutes, breathing in circles to remain calm. I rubbed my hands on my pants. They didn't dry up. Then the shorthaired waitress strode over to me, looking like she had something to say. Good, maybe she's going to tell me that Elena is still in the restroom and we can order. Or maybe it was some sort of girl thing that the waitress had caught on to and was now going to fill me in.

"You Shimeon, right?" she said.

"Close enough."

"You have a phone call."

"Okay, thank you," I said.

A phone call? Who knew I was here? Maybe it was Peter and he was drunk and wanted to tell me a funny story about tractors. I walked over to the phone on the wall. Three of the cooks were now eating their lunch together. You know, when the help eats at Chinese restaurants they never serve normal dishes, or at least not dishes I have ever seen anyone else eat. Maybe the secret recipes were located near those secret showers. I made a note to ask our shorthaired waitress later. Note taken.

"Hello."

"Simeon," a man's voice said.

"Yeah."

"This is B.D. over at the gym."

I started shaking and felt ready to vomit.

"Hi, B.D., what's going on?" I asked, hoping with all my might that nothing was going on.

"I'm calling for Elena," he said. "She asked me to call you and say that she had to go but maybe she can call you later."

"She had to go?" I asked.

"Yeah, Simeon," he said. "What's your phone number?"

I gave it to him in a daze. The Ecuadorian harlot had abandoned me smack dab in the middle of the Chinese Kingdom. I was on the phone. Everyone was watching. I didn't know what to do. I had to get out of there fast. So I told the shorthaired waitress that my date was ill and I had to go. She smiled. I smiled and walked away back to get my white car in the parking lot of Pure USA.

Wouldn't you know, it fired right up. I think it sensed that I was confused and sad, and I was. I couldn't help but wonder what I had said to Elena that made her leave. I was so careful not to say anything that could be misconstrued on the entire walk to the Kingdom, then when we had just sat down, she vanished. Maybe I shouldn't have been so bold and asked her out so fast, when I don't know the first thing about her. She was so beautiful. She was also nervous around me, which made me think that she wanted to see me again.

I went on with my life for the next couple of weeks, continued with my Greek classes at night and went to work and talked to Peter on a daily basis. Then one night, when I was taking a shower, the phone rang. It was her. I could sense it from the way the water pressure went from strong to soft and then I was scorched by hot water. It could have been someone next door flushing the toilet, but I think it was the fact that the Ecuadorian princess had come to her senses and was leaving a message on my machine. My skin was red on my back and I didn't dry off completely before I put on my boxers and a long-sleeved blue T-shirt. There was a message.

"Hi, Simeon, this is Elena. Um, I'm really sorry about the other day, actually it was a couple of weeks ago. I'm sorry it took me so long to call you back, but anyway, call me if you can, when you get this message, and maybe we can meet for coffee or something. I haven't seen you at Pure USA lately, either. I was hoping to catch you there. Oh, also, the Pure Retreat is this coming weekend and I'm going and I think Alan will be there if you want to come. It is $120 for the weekend in Santa Ynez at a winery and spa place called Casa Llena and that includes all activities and food and stuff. We're taking a van on Friday at 4:00. Anyway, call me either way. Bye."

I wish I was an opera singer and fat. Because at this point I would belt out, in perfect Italian, my feelings and pain and concern and angst and it would sound to you like the cries of an aging father sending off his young son to battle the barbarians. At least that's what you would think, because you don't speak or read Italian. Go ahead and think that, but really I would be singing about insecurity, Elena, fear and my almost suicidal inclination to take chances with people. Either way it would sound good but feel terrible.

Against all good judgment, I called the 800 number for Pure USA Gym and signed up for the weekend. It couldn't be that bad, not if the Ecuadorian Artist was going to be there, and I loved wine. It would give me a chance to over-drink and ask Alan if he still had that bottle of vodka in his trunk and about his parents. Then after another glass of wine I would listen to Elena explain to me that she left the restaurant because her body was going into convulsions due to the passion she felt for me. It was my smell, my very essence that drove her insane. So, she fled, refusing to begin the relationship without control. I couldn't blame her.

CHAPTER 3

I packed my bag on Thursday night and found my journal from a trip I had taken to Ecuador in college. I thought I would bring it to give Elena and me a conversation topic. I parked my white Swedish chariot for the weekend and made my way over to the dark blue van. It was going to be the strangest weekend I have ever spent at a winery in Santa Ynez. In fact, it was the start of many strange weekends.

I was one of the first to arrive, so I got in the van and went straight to the back for a better perspective. I was sitting back there, nervous, when Elena walked in with wet hair and smelling like a field of gardenias. She was completely moisturized from head to toe. She continued walking until she reached me, smiled and said, "Hi, Simeon, I'm glad you decided to join us."

"Yeah, great, thanks," I said, the best I could come up with on short notice.

"I'm the navigator, so I can't sit next to you, but we can talk later," she said.

Yeah. We can talk later.

The drive was uneventful, except for the fact that everyone in the car except me smelled like a tropical jungle. B.D. was driving and wore cop glasses and drank water constantly. I began to think that there was a good chance he was a real bastard.

When we finally pulled up to the Casa Llena four muscular men in tank tops were waiting to greet us in front of what looked like an old barn. They smelled like Old Spice. They helped us with our bags and then said, almost in unison, "The Pure Air class starts in five, so drop off your bags, put on some workout clothes and head out."

Great. What the hell is a Pure Air class? I wanted wine. I wanted cheese. I began to look around frantically for any Chinese people. Maybe they could save me from this torture and ride me on their handlebars to freedom and a shower. I didn't see anyone. There were just six of us in the van: Elena, Alan, a guy named Vic and his wife Kara, B.D. and me. I changed and dropped my stuff off in the room they assigned me, which was light blue with lots of light. The bed was small and there were five candles waiting to be lit. This could be the site of my tryst with Elena.

I made my way into the barn. There was steam and, again, the four men, who were now wearing headsets and standing up front by the beautiful barrels of Pinot Noir and Cabernet. The music began, slowly, cautiously. Boom. Boom. Boomboom. Piano. Strings. Boom. Boomboom.

"Okay, people, close your eyes and jump. Now. Now. Yes. Jump."

I began to jump. We all were jumping. Up and down. The four Spice Boys were yelling at us to jump more. Push the envelope. Rewire your enzymes. Work hard. Jump. Jump. A few times when I was in midair I began to question my sanity and my propensity for getting mixed up with groups of odd people. But that thought disappeared as I was being yelled at by a tanning salon worshiper with huge calves. "Higher. Higher."

Finally, the jumping was over and we were commanded to shower up and meet in the barn for dinner and a class on personality types. If they didn't serve wine, I would steal the van and head back to civilization and report the group to the Better Business Bureau.

After I showered, I walked to the barn, eagerly anticipating seeing Elena and beginning the rest of my life with her. The barn was lit with candles and I could smell the wine. Thank God. The wine. I was the last to sit down and when I did, the bastard with the cop glasses walked up to me with a small stack of papers stapled together and said in a whisper, "Simeon, we are all filling out this personality test and when we're done, I will go over the results and then we will all talk about it." Great. A test, in the middle of a barn full of wine. My heart began to sink.

I took the papers and the pencil and began answering the questions. There were three sections: Body, Mind and Spirit. I started with Body; at this point in my life, in terms of mass, I would have the most confidence answering questions about my body. The questions were odd. Like, "Do your shoulders droop when you walk into a room?" Or, "Do you notice your heart rate increasing when you walk into an amusement park?" Or, "Do you feel like your genitals really belong to you, or do you feel as if they are on loan from a distant relative?" I was convinced that bastard B.D. wrote that one. He, no doubt, is a sexual Olympian, in stature and stamina.

They continued, "Do you bite your nails?" "Do you enjoy being touched on the hand or forehead by close friends?" I was beginning to wish I was at a tractor pull in Kansas. I answered the questions as honestly as possible because, in the back of my mind, I felt that maybe I could learn something about myself. I moved on to the Spirit section. There were such questions as, "Do you associate the wind with the holy spirit or a natural occurrence?" and "Do you feel lonely when you are in a room for more than an hour and no one says your name?" Or "Have you ever felt like your lot in life was nothing, you were going nowhere and nobody, including yourself, cared at all?" My favorite one was, "If someone criticizes you, do you get defensive or do you listen, think and then thank them for their insight?" I wanted to write, "It depends" for almost every question except the one about the wind. I love the wind, especially the warm Santa Ana winds that blow through Southern California in late fall. I finished the twenty questions in the Spirit section and then moved onto the Mind section.

"When you close your eyes and look into your stomach, is it all black and charred?" Or "When you were a teenager did you write your name on your notebook, over and over again, and did you find that you took longer showers?" The questions were, oddly, non-religious. There were no questions about sincere relationships with

God, or the attempt to seek out God and begin a relationship. They all revolved around concepts of soul and God and spirit, without any concrete, traditional foundations. I answered as best I could and handed in my paper, anxious to get to the garlic, pasta and wine. The bastard took the forms and walked out of the barn. He probably doesn't need to eat. It gets in the way of his workouts and tanning salon visits.

We now had some free time while the men in headsets had secret meetings. I went for a walk outside the barn. I could see what looked like miles and miles of grapevines, all lined up in perfect rows. I wondered how they get them all lined up correctly and then keep them that way. I had seen a vineyard before, but have never seen anyone working on the vines, picking or plucking or whatever it is that they do. I continued to walk on, feeling alone, like I was in the process of making a big mistake with nowhere to go. I tried to take some deep breaths and continued walking. I was also thinking about the history of wine and all the people who have ever enjoyed the effects of a tall glass of red wine and aren't around to enjoy it again. Someday, I realized, I won't be able to either. That is a difficult thought for me—the idea that I will someday die and no longer be able to see Elena, or to write articles about tractors, talk to my friends, see my mom, wonder about my dad and go to strange gyms run by tanned maniacs. Really, the idea that I will someday be lying in a grave truly bothers me. It will happen to all of us sooner or later. It's just that we all wish it would come later, much later. Some people say that you should be looking at your shoulder every morning, at the little bird sitting there, and asking him, "Is today the day?" Well, if today is the day then I would really like to have some dinner first. Dinner that included Elena and wine and a respite from the tanned Olympian. I'll put money on the fact that B.D., like Michael Jackson, has come up with a plan to beat death. He probably has one of those cryogenic machines in the back room of Pure USA.

I made it back to the barn and I noticed six individual tables, each with a candle and a stack of papers. I sat and looked around, astonished that we were not all sitting together. Elena was nowhere to be found. I spotted Alan, who appeared to have hit the wine supply earlier than the rest of us, and I waved at him. He was acting oddly. He waved back with a guilty look on his face. Then Mr. Immortal walked in and stood in front of us all, closing his eyes and taking loud, deep breaths, holding in the air for a few seconds and then expelling it through his nose. I could smell him from my seat, twenty feet away.

"Welcome everyone. I hope you all are situated in your rooms and ready to make some drastic changes. You may notice that you are sitting alone. We do this for a reason, which you will find out later. This weekend, I want you to know, will change your life. You will never be the same. You will learn things about yourself that will make your life more fulfilling, more real, more connected. Usually we do this weekend with groups of at least twenty, but the smaller the group the better, actually. It will give you more time to get it.

What the hell? Can't we just eat dinner? Where was Elena?

31

He continued. "I need a commitment from you right now. I need to know that you are going to give me and the other volunteers the truth. You are going to give us you. You are going to follow all our rules. If you don't, you will be asked to leave. I need to know that you are here of your own doing and that you are here because you want to change. You want to grow. You will go through this weekend and experience amazing emotions. You will feel sick. You might get the shakes. Some of you will become physically ill and even vomit on yourselves. You are going to cleanse yourself, and that cleansing will trigger some resistance from your body and spirit. But you must trust me and the other volunteers. If you don't, you will not fully let go and get it. I need you to tell us right now if you are willing to continue. Say 'I am' now and we will proceed."

Along with the others, I replied, "I am," meanwhile picturing Alan throwing up on himself in the corner like he did that night in college. I didn't really want to barf in front of Elena, but they do that a lot in Ecuador, so maybe she was used to it. I threw up when I was in Ecuador last time, but that was because I had a parasite that took up residence in my intestines. That had nothing to do with the fact that I was building up a great hatred for B.D. and the rest of the soldiers with microphones. He continued on.

"Okay. We are all committed. Now I will go over the rules."

He closed his eyes like he was praying and did the breathing thing again.

"No one leaves this room until I or a volunteer say it is okay. It is 8:15 in the evening. You will have a break every two hours. Then

32

and only then will you be able to leave this room. You will not be eating tonight. If you don't like that you can leave right now. No snacking. You will abstain from alcohol, drugs and sex this entire weekend. You will be honest with everyone here. If you want to say something you will raise your hand and someone will bring you a microphone. You may not leave your table, stand up, lie on the floor or stretch until the break. If you don't like any of these rules you can leave right now."

I wanted to leave. I should have, looking back on the entire weekend. But I think I stuck it out for Elena, wherever she was. Besides, I was at a point in my life where some self-realization might do some good. So I thought. I was so hungry. A part of me, though, trusted B.D. and this whole Jump weekend. I don't know what it was about Elena, but I felt this connection with her. It had been almost two years since I had been in a relationship that lasted more than a month and I think for some reason I was finally ready to get to know someone, to try to love someone. Anyway, I didn't leave, even though I had to go to the bathroom. I was mad and confused. Why did the bastard put us in a room full of wine barrels and tell us we couldn't eat or drink any alcohol? What did he mean by get it?

"Are there any questions?" he asked.

Vic raised his hand. One of the microphoned mercenaries strode over to him and told him to state his name.

"My name is Vic and I have a question. My wife and I are hungry and we think you are all a bunch of self-righteous fanatics. We came up here to lose some weight and get away from our kids. Now you

33

tell us we're going to puke on each other and then you deny us food and drink. We're not happy. In, fact we're downright pissed." He sat down. B.D. responded.

"Good, Vic. I share with you. But, I disagree. You'll get it if you want it."

"Get what?" Vic yelled.

"Be quiet," B.D. said. "You will only respond into the microphone and when you are called on. Now shut up and realize that you and your wife and everyone in this room are idiots. You don't know who you are, what you want, where you are going or who you want to be."

Now I was beginning to really hate the tanned bastard. I wanted to move my stupid table over to the side of the room where Vic and Kara were sitting to form some kind of band of solidarity. But, according to the rules, we weren't allowed to leave our seats. The whole time he was calling us idiots I was trying to figure out his strategy. I think he was trying to break us down, get us to where we were really vulnerable and then fill us up with good stuff. Bad stuff out, good stuff in. I hadn't thrown up yet. Elena was nowhere to be found. B.D. continued.

"And you, Alan. You of all people are an idiot. You've done similar jump training before, and you still don't get it. Why don't you get it, Alan?"

Alan raised his hand and was given a microphone.

"I share with you, leader, but I disagree with you."

"If you get it, why are you twenty pounds overweight and full of guilt and low self-esteem, you idiot?" B.D. shouted.

"I share with you, leader, and agree that I am overweight and have low self-esteem. I want to do better and feel better," Alan said, and then sat down. I saw a candy bar wrapper peeking out of his pocket and I wanted to cause some kind of diversion so the soldiers didn't find out that he may have been snacking. I raised my hand and said:

"I'm hungry and I would like some wine. I appreciate what you're trying to do, but I think we would all make just as much progress if you allowed us to eat and sip some of this nice wine that they make here."

B.D. responded. "I share that and I disagree with you. You are not permitted to eat and drink because it is part of your cleansing process. When you are denied what you want, you find out what you really need. Maybe you don't get it because you are fat and don't have the strength to do anything about it."

I looked around the room to see if my princess was listening but I didn't see her. I began to shake with anger and I wanted to hurt B.D. Instead, I just raised my hand. The goons brought me the microphone of doom again.

"You know what? I am overweight. In fact, I'm a little stocky. I share that. And, to your surprise, I'm sure, I get it. That's why I'm here. The real question is, B.D, not why we are here, but why you and the rest of your posse do these weekend retreats?" Everyone looked down at the ground. There was silence. I overdid it. B.D. sat down, grabbed the microphone and said smugly, "I share that. And, I understand the question. I will talk more about that later. For now, before we lose focus, I want all of you idiots to refer to the papers on your table. They will have three letters on the front that represent something. I want to go around the room and have you tell me who you are.

Vic said, "SFO." Kara said, "SFW." Alan said, "MFP." And, I said "TFB."

Peter had told me about these personality tests. Companies that are having trouble with their employees hire people like B.D. to come in and devise and administer these tests. They tabulate and interpret the results and from that they analyze and evaluate the employees, letting them know who they really are, so they can work better at realizing their full potential and, more importantly, making the company more money. This self-realization policy also has other effects. When someone says something that hurts you or seems competitive or petty, you can say to yourself, "That's okay, she is just a PPP and that's the only way she knows how to express herself." Then your feelings won't be hurt and you can get back to making the company more money, knowing that there is a simple little system that categorizes people into little boxes. Once you know the box you fit in, you will never be sad or unhappy or mad again. And the company will show their appreciation for all the extra money you've made them by giving you a T-shirt.

Mr. Skin Cancer continued.

"The first letter of your personality type represents your Body. The second letter represents your Mind and the third your Spirit. This test has been given to thousands of people around the country and was created by five famous psychologists and sociologists in New York. You can trust it. It works. It will help you get it."

He went on to describe all of us by our three letter tags.

"Vic, since you are an SFO that means you are Short in body, Feeble in mind and an Orange in Spirit. I will explain what they all mean in a minute.

"Kara, you are an SFW. That means you are Short in body, Feeble in mind and a Watermelon in Spirit. No wonder you two got married." Vic and Kara weren't sure if that was a compliment or an insult so they just looked at each other as if they were planning an escape.

"Alan, you are a MFP. That means you are Medium in body, Feeble in mind and a Peach in spirit. And Simeon, you are a TFB, which means you are Tall in body, Feeble in mind and a Banana in Spirit," he said.

Great, so we are a bunch of feeble fruits. Where was Elena? Where were the bikes? I needed a great escape. Maybe a band of angry Chinese restaurant owners would appear on bicycles and peddle us away on their handlebars. Then, because they felt sorry for us, they would not only show us where they shower, but they would serve us the secret dishes that they serve each other. Then we would all shoot off firecrackers and dance in circles wearing wooden shoes. Arm in arm.

B.D. walked over to some big white board and wrote this:

Body

Short—short arms and legs, limited ass and stout chest

Medium—medium arms and legs, medium ass and fat chest

Tall—long arms and legs, big ass and no chest

Mind

Feeble—no discipline, run by emotions, feeler as opposed to thinker

Fanciful—Disciplined, regimented, practical, thinker as opposed to feeler

Spirit

Orange—Thick skin, sweet on the inside but potent, healthy and needed by all

Watermelon—Too big. Lots of sweet meat but full of little black things

Peach—Thin skin, sweet, elegant, powerfully deceptive and true

Banana—Thick skin, long, dense, helpful and sweet

He instructed us all to look up at the board and notice where we fit in and think about some of our habits and tendencies. He began to do that breathing thing again with his eyes closed. I thought before that he might be praying, but now I know he wasn't. It is impossible to pray to yourself, but that was the only entity that B.D. was going to pray to.

"Okay, idiots, remain in your seats. We are going to make some fruit salad." Vic and Kara looked at each other like they were going to break down and cry. Out of the corner of my eye I noticed Alan curling up in his chair. Then, like the splash of the Log Jam ride at Disneyland, he erupted. He vomited all over his shoes and onto the ground. He had both hands around his stomach.

"Good, you idiot." B.D. smiled. Vic got up from his chair and started walking toward him, his eyes ablaze with anger. Two of the goons grabbed him and hustled him back to his seat. I wasn't quite sure why Alan was vomiting. He looked like he had hit the wine earlier.

"Alan, even though he is an idiot, is getting it. He is purging, cleansing. While the rest of you sit here and hate me and the other volunteers, you are just wasting energy. You see, it isn't about us. It is about you. And what you do with you. And who you are when you are YOU. And why you are when you are you and with whom. Get it?"

Apparently I did. I threw up. Either that, or the stench of Alan's puking finally got to me.

Vic got it, too.

And because B.D. felt like we needed to digest more of "who we were and why we didn't get it," he let us go to bed a little early and said that after the morning exercise class, we would move onto chanting, then resume the Fruit Salad exercise. We were all dejected and confused. Poor Kara looked like she was having flashbacks from college and Vic was in a post-purging depression. I didn't know what to do, so I got up from my chair, patted Alan on the shoulder and walked toward my room. I was planning on going to bed, but when I walked in my door, my plans changed.

Elena was sitting on my bed.

And she was shaking and crying. I walked over to her, knelt beside her, put my hand on her back and tried to console her.

"I'm sorry to be here," she said.

"Don't be sorry. I'm glad you're here. And I'm glad I left that bizarre training session," I said.

"You didn't like the training, huh?" she asked, concerned.

"No, not much. I know now that I can vomit in a group and that I am fat, an idiot and bear a strong resemblance to a fruit. I'm glad you told me about this weekend, Elena."

She laughed and got up and said, "I'll be right back, stay here."

I watched her leave the room with that perfect walk of hers. Her dark skin glistened regally, and the combination of the way she smelled as she passed by me and the knowledge that not only was she in my room when I got there but that she was coming back caused my stomach to do more gymnastic maneuvers. When she walked out I grabbed some stuff from my bag and cleaned up a little bit—actually, a lot. I brushed my teeth, cleaned my face, put my head under the sink, slapped on some aftershave and changed my shirt. It all took about a minute and I returned to my bed and sat down to wait for my Xena.

I waited for three hours.

At least I think it was three hours. I had fallen asleep, woken up and slipped under the covers to go to sleep again, hoping she had gotten roped in by B.D. and his Golden Horde and had done to her what had been done to us. Yes, I was just a tad angry. I knew if I ever saw her again I would let her know exactly what I thought of her.

Which is exactly what I didn't do when she woke me up at 4:00 in the morning.

"Simeon. I'm sorry to wake you up. I got stuck with B.D.," she said.

"That's okay." I sat up on the bed and surreptitiously slipped into my mouth a mint that I had strategically placed on the table by the bed in case this very thing happened. Good planning. Good thinking.

"Simeon, I have to tell you. You are so sweet and kind and funny and I like you a lot, but you don't want to go out with a girl like me. You really don't need to get mixed up with someone like me. You need a kind, sweet girl who will take care of you," she said, tears welling up in her eyes.

"I don't know what you mean, Elena. I WANT to get mixed up with you, and I like you, too." I leaned over and kissed her and she put her hand on my waist and started moving it toward my lower back. Then her other hand.

It was a mysterious kiss. Time stopped. Then she stood up and said, "Simeon, I can't do this. You don't want to get to know me. I have to go."

I grabbed her arm and pulled her toward me.

"Elena, I do want to get to know you. Tell me what you're worried about."

She began to tremble a little and gazed up at me. In a tone that seemed like it was almost do or die, she said, "You don't know all

41

there is to know about this gym. You don't know all there is to know about B.D. and the group and the others. Some of it is good, but some of it is bad, very, very bad. And I'm involved. And there are bad things involved, and I'm with B.D."

That was it. She was with B.D. I turned my back and walked toward the far end of the small room. I could hear her shaking and crying. That was why he called me at the Chinese Kingdom. I was mad at her and mad at B.D., but the whole thing made me feel even more attracted to her. I walked back over to her and held her and put my hand on the back of her head and pulled it toward my chest. She seemed so helpless in my arms. She was so small. We stayed in that position for a long time and then I pushed her slowly away from me and kissed her again and I could taste the residue of tears in her mouth and feel her moist cheeks against mine. I wanted to stay there for a long time. Then the image of B.D. popped into my head, and I again heard him say that we had to abstain from any intimate activity this weekend. Well, you monumental fitness freak, I'm gonna break that rule. What were you doing to her and what were you doing to the rest of us? If you touch this girl that I now have in my arms one more time I will rent a Caterpillar 9400 and drive it straight through your faux-Sharper Image-decorated house stuffed with the latest useless gadgets. Don't touch this girl again and don't come anywhere near me or I will injure you. Somehow. Maybe the training was working?

I held on to Elena. It seemed as if I needed her just as much as she needed me. And now it was early in the morning and her eyes were closed and she was in my arms and I walked her over to the bed and sat down, still holding on to her, and then put my back on the bed and held her on top of me. I grabbed the blanket and pulled it over her body and put my fingers through the back of her hair. We both fell asleep.

We were probably only asleep for a few hours when there was a knock at the door.

"Simeon. Wake up. Be in the barn in fifteen minutes for Empathy Class," said B.D. Then I heard the door handle turn, but thank God I had locked it when I got up for some water in the middle of our slumber. Elena woke up but she didn't seem as alarmed as I was that B.D. was five feet away from us. She wanted him to come in and see us. I know that now, but I didn't know that then. I knew only two things that morning. One, I was in love with a small Ecuadorian woman and two, I had to escape this loony bin and get myself back home to my apartment. Elena sat up and I could smell her on my shirt. Her attitude, however, was a bit different than it had been just a few hours before.

"I have to go, Simeon, "she said, coarsely, like we did this all the time.

"Okay," I answered. She got up and went into the bathroom, closing the door behind her. A few minutes later she came out and, without a word to me or even an acknowledgement that I was there, she crossed the room to the door and walked right out. I kept thinking I was going to hear B.D. screaming at her and then he was going to charge into my room and impale me, but nothing happened. I grabbed my cell phone out of my bag and dialed Peter. He answered.

43

"Peter, this is Simeon."

"What's wrong, Sim?"

"I'm trapped in a self-help conference, I threw up last night and I'm in love with the instructor's girlfriend. In fact, she spent last night in my room. Peter, you have to come get me. I have to make an escape," I pleaded.

"I suppose now wouldn't be a good time to mention that I told you I thought going there this weekend was a bad idea," he reminded me. Peter had been a volunteer with EST for almost three years until he finally got it and left.

"No, it wouldn't," I replied, smiling to myself.

I gave him directions, and with the assurance that only a best friend can provide, he told me he would meet me in two hours at the gate to the entrance of the ranch. I thanked him and got my bags ready. I had to kill some time, however, so I decided to go to the Empathy Class; when we all came back to shower, I would make my escape.

I walked down to the barn with Vic and Kara, who looked like they needed a friend like Peter. In a reckless moment of compassion I told them of my plan and asked if they wanted to make the escape with me. They most certainly did. We all were rejuvenated. My fear of the escape was tempered by my hatred of the tanning salon bastard and his devious plans. Although I didn't know what they were, I was convinced they were devious and that he was holding Elena hostage as his lover and the only way I would ever free her was to let him know I was not on his side. I was forming a rebel army. We were starting a guerrilla war—oddly enough, we were rebelling against an authority we had paid to be with. In any case, I had now recruited two other rebels and our first mission was to escape the self-help conference intact. First, though, we had to endure a little Empathy.

We walked into the barn, which was decorated with pink balloons. There were baby pictures on the walls. The music was different. B.D.'s storm troopers were wearing purple sweat suits and holding strange looking objects in their arms. We all gathered together. Alan looked tired.

"Good morning, everyone," said one of our captors.

"Good morning," we shouted back.

"Welcome to Empathy Class. This morning we are all pregnant women. All of us."

He handed each of us this strap-on thing that they called an empathy belly and we helped each other Velcro the heavy fabric thing to our backs and stomachs.

"Once you put on the bellies, line up and imagine that you are pregnant women."

This was not good. Here I was in the middle of a civil war and the enemy was strapping fake stomachs with fake babies on us and telling us to pretend we are pregnant women. Is this necessary?

We lined up and walked outside the barn. I could hear the thumping music beginning. Boom. Boomboom. Strings. Strings. Boom. Boomboom.

"Now prance, flap your arms like birds. Keep prancing. Squats. Leg kicks. Flap your arms. Now prance. Keep moving, ladies. You're pregnant but still in shape."

Here we were, four people with empathy bellies strapped on us, prancing around a winery. I wish Peter could have seen this.

"Keep moving, ladies. How does it feel to be pregnant?" the soldier yelled.

"Heavy," responded Alan. I looked over at Vic and Kara and, with a nod, we sealed the commitment to our escape. No more exercise classes, no more fruit salad. We continued to prance.

When the hour was over they took off our empathy bellies and let us return to our rooms to shower. I spoke to my two co-conspirators on the way in. We planned to shower up, grab our stuff and rendezvous at the front gate at 10:00. I thought about putting face paint on and taping bushes and flowers to my head for camo, but I didn't do it. I grabbed my stuff, hoped Peter would be on time and sneaked out the door of the room. When I got into the open yard I started running. Slowly at first, and then at a good clip, I ran towards the gate at the entrance to the ranch.

I was halfway there when I spotted a pink, 1963 Thunderbird— Peter's mom's car! I continued to run and heard some yelling from behind me, but I was too nervous to turn around for fear that B.D and the other morons were going to run me down in a Hummer. I looked back anyway and saw Vic and Kara running at full speed with all their bags bouncing up and down, and two men walking fast behind them; our escape had been detected! I was closing on the car and began to get that feeling in my stomach that I had the night before when the queen of the world was asleep in my arms. I wondered if she would ever again spend a night in a bed with me. I hoped so. I don't remember ever sleeping that well with any other overnight guest. As I got closer to the car I yelled to Peter to fire it up; he did, and I threw my stuff in the trunk and we waited anxiously for Vic and Kara to make it to the Thunderbird. Only, they didn't make it.

Evidently, Vic wasn't in the best of shape and all the prancing around with empathy belly intact had pretty much worn him out. I looked back and Kara now had both bags in her hands and the bad men were right on their tails.

"Should we drive down the road and pick them up?" I asked Peter. He shook his head.

Then I heard Kara yell, "Go ahead Simeon, take off while you can, we'll be all right."

Vic was already talking to the bad men and I don't think Kara wanted to leave him there alone. I guess they were destined to be fruit salad with Alan. I, on the other hand, was going to plan a way to rescue my heroine from the devious plot of B.D and the rest of them.

"Let's go," I said to Peter, and off we went toward the Santa Ynez Valley in our salvific pink Ford Thunderbird.

CHAPTER 4

Monday morning Peter and I were in the office and I was pretty quiet. I didn't want to talk much about the weekend. I couldn't stop smelling Elena and tasting her tears in my mouth and feeling her tremble against my chest. For once I felt like I was really needed, that I could help her and give her a chance in life. Something like that, anyway. Maybe I was just infatuated with her skin and her voice and her body and all. Deep breath.

Newsstand sales of the last two issues of *Man Tractors* were down, which was unusual for the spring season. Peter decided we needed to appeal to a broader audience of tractor lovers and shake up the next issue a bit. That meant I got to write three short, general-interest stories that still involved tractors and the men who love them. The first story I was going to write was a glory piece on the machine/tractor that cut a 31-mile tunnel across the English Channel connecting Cheriton, England, with Sangatte, France. The article was going to canonize the machine and include diagrams and pictures.

And so I began.

The question has to be asked by every red-blooded American, every guy who clogs his arteries with chicken-fried steak and barbecue sauce: "Why would anyone in their right mind want to be able to drive from England to France through a tunnel?" Would you? Well, probably not (me either), but apparently a large portion of the British population thought it was an important venture. I guess too much tea tends to make people foggy. Regardless of why the Chunnel—as it is now called—was built, what makes it an interesting story is the machine and the men who built it.

There was an attempt to build the tunnel back in 1881, but the English axed the project and it wasn't until the late 1970s that the idea was proposed again. The tunnel project began officially in 1987 and was completed in 1994. Now to the good stuff. Imagine a giant concrete and metal worm with enough power and might that could conceivably, if allowed to run wild, dig to the core of the earth and send the planet careening towards Pluto before we could say "Dijon." The Chunnel was built using eleven tunnel-boring machines (TBMs) with 26-foot cutter heads and eight arms studded with cutting picks and discs. It took 15,000 workers to remove 283 million cubic feet of dirt and chalk. The entire project cost in the neighborhood of fifteen billion dollars.

I have to say it: that's a lot of tea and crumpets. Workers began on both ends of the channel and worked seven days a week for seven years until the TBMs ran into each other under the cold English Channel. The Chunnel consists of three parallel tunnels thirty one miles in length. There are two main tunnels that boast a twenty-five-foot diameter that were built for high-speed trains and a tunnel in between for service projects. That's a big hole in the ground. Kudos to the Euros for moving a heck of a lot of dirt, but as for me, I'd rather drive an RV to the Grand Canyon and look at what God can do when He puts the hammer down.

Peter wasn't sure about the story, but he was still sort of angry about having to rescue me Saturday, so I didn't take it to heart. I was

49

working on a few other stories, but I took a walk to get some lunch and ended up at the library to check out *A Greek Commentary on the Gospel of Mathew*. I had been translating that for one of my classes at the City College. New Testament Greek and especially the Gospel of Matthew is a good place to start, because the structure and vocabulary is fairly straightforward. While I was there I got on the computer and just for fun did a search for "Pure USA Gym" to see if the bastards had a web page. Lo and behold, they did—and guess whose picture was on the opening page? My lover. My woman. What was she doing? I clicked on "What we are about" and found out something very interesting. They started out not with a history of the gym, but with a history of B.D. According to the web page. B.D. is Hawaiian, "a direct descendant of the Menehune peoples who inhabited the Hawaiian Islands in ancient times." What does that mean? The text went on to relate how the Menehune had reached legendary and even mythical status in Polynesian history and that, although they were very short in stature and had abnormally large abdomens, they performed miraculous feats of strength and engineering, working only at night and for the price of one shrimp per person. So that was why he was so small. I'm convinced he's Italian. My anger was welling up inside of me. He probably gave Elena that Menehune story, too, so she thinks he is part of this famous family of people. What could I do?

I checked out a few books on Polynesian culture and the history of the islands to find out more about this race and B.D.'s alleged claim to fame so I could bring it up with him the next time I saw him.

I picked up a cup of coffee and began walking back to the office when I saw a woman who looked just like my mom. I almost stopped and said something to her, but when she turned around I realized it wasn't her. I hadn't seen my mom in almost two years. She was still living in our hometown of Richardton, North Dakota, where she ran a home for runaway kids called the Hope House. She started the home after I left to go to college and now she had ten to fifteen kids living with her at all times. She is almost 70 years old. The home has become such a success that she even had to hire some full-time help. I don't know what it is about her, but whenever her image pops into my head I get this overwhelming feeling of kindness. I haven't been dealt the most perfect hand in life, but I thank God every day that I had a mother who covered up most of the confusion of childhood with a warm and kind blanket of courage.

She calls me every month to talk about the stories I write in *Man Tractors* and tells me about the kids she's trying to help. I think she's proud of me, of the fact that I'm a writer and that I'm taking classes at night. I wonder if she would like Elena. I think she would. She would look her over for a few minutes like mothers do and then her compassion would come through and she would take her hand and ask her to come inside and sit down. Then she would sit next to her, like mothers sit, with her legs together to one side, and say, "So tell me dear, how did you and Simeon meet?" I could picture Elena shaking a little bit and fumbling with her words. I don't think my mom would like the whole B.D. thing.

51

I'm glad my mom is not around my dad anymore. She's way too good for him. But I know deep in my heart that one of the reasons she loves me so much is that I look and sound and act just like he did before everything fell apart.

Something happened to her after I left. It was almost as if she slowly but surely became the woman she always wanted to be. It took her a few years to shed the vestiges of her former life with my dad, but, when she finally did, she transformed into an independent, courageous woman with a fervent desire to help children who had lost their way. She was helped by St. Joseph's Parish in Richardton. Father Michael would come by every week to spend time counseling the kids. I think he also helped my mom out with some of the financing for the home. They had become good friends over the years and she speaks of him as if they have known each other their whole lives.

I got back to work and Peter was sitting in his chair, going over my story, and, with a somewhat concerned look, he handed me a note.

"Elena called. She sounded upset," he said. "I told her you'd call her right back."

"Thanks," I replied.

I went back to my desk with my heart beating just like it did when I saw her sitting on my bed at the retreat. I wondered why she was upset and why she wanted to talk to me. My stomach hurt but it was a good hurt, and it occurred to me that whenever I was thinking about Elena, I wasn't as hungry as usual. Maybe love was the diet I needed;

maybe I could stay away from the endorphin junkies at the gym and remain sedentary as long as I was fantasizing about my Xena.

I dialed her number.

"Hello," she sang.

"Hey, this is Simeon."

"Hi, Siiimeon," she said, just like that.

"Hi, Elena. What's going on?"

"I need your help, Simeon," she said.

"Okay. What do you need?" I asked.

"Well, I'm in a little bit of trouble," she said, lowering her voice.

"What can I do?" I asked.

"Can you come down to Pure USA?"

"Is B.D there?"

"No, it's just me."

"Okay. I'll come right down."

I told Peter I was going to go see Elena. He looked at me like a father looks at his son who has just walked through the front door at 3:00 in the morning after having been told to be home by midnight.

"Don't lose yourself in her, Simeon," he warned. "You don't really know her yet."

I nodded, but didn't take it to heart; who listens to advice about relationships anyway? I've noticed that when someone gives me advice about a girl I'm interested in, I can hear their words coming through my ears, but the words dissolve without having any effect on me at all.

53

As I was walking into Pure USA I got the feeling that perhaps I was getting into something that might just turn out to be something I didn't want to get into. Instead of turning back, though, I grabbed the Gothic doors with my sweaty palms and went right through. I saw Elena standing behind the desk. She saw me and averted her eyes. She was wearing these orange sweat/fashion pants, a white workout top and a sweatshirt tied around her waist.

"Hey, Sim," she said as I walked up to her.

She kissed me on the cheek, grabbing my hand at the same time. She didn't mention the sweat on my palms. I fell in love with her all over again. She led me into the back where all the sweatshirts and T-shirts were stacked. She slid her hands around my waist, put her head into my chest, then looked up at me and said, "You have no idea how much I want to be with you."

I didn't know what to say.

"You are too good for me, Simeon. I don't deserve you."

"You do deserve me," I said. "Just like I deserve you."

"I have to tell you again, Sim. You don't know what you're getting into."

She turned away, her fingers still holding mine. And then, a small bomb went off.

"Elena, are you in back?"

It was B.D.

"Yeah, B.D., Hold on a minute."

"You have to go," she said. "Go out this back door. Quickly. I'll call you later."

I ran out the back door, through the parking lot and made my way back to the front of the building, completely confused. Did she want to get caught? Why did I have to go down there?

I walked back to work and Peter didn't say anything when I came in. I think he knew what was going on. Thankfully, he let me be.

I sat down and started researching the second of the three articles on amazing machines. This one was on a giant dump truck called the Komatsu 930E.

And so, dejected and confused, I began,

It is the largest truck in the world. Almost thirty feet long, it is twenty-six feet wide and eight feet deep. Want to go swimming? Don't think so. We're not talking about a community pool—you know, the kind where you have to pay $3.00 to swim in a vat of kids' urine, a place that sounds like an avalanche, where everyone is either sunburned or in the twenty-fifth minute of a thirty-minute waiting period to let their food digest. Lucky bastards. If they only knew. No, we're talking about the Komatsu 930E. The $3.6-million, 310-ton monster mover, whose engine puts out 2500 roaring, snorting horsepower, whose crankcase takes fifty-five gallons of oil to fill and whose fuel tank holds 1200 gallons of diesel. Big enough for ya?

And so on.

Peter read it and told me to go home and get some rest. I did.

When I got home I ate fifteen pieces of turkey ham, had some chocolate, chips and salsa and a coke. Then I sat on the couch and put on some music. The Buggles. *The Age of Plastic.* Simply the greatest album made. Video did kill the radio star. It was the very first video on MTV and while I sat there eating Captain Crunch and memorizing all the information on the left hand bottom of the screen before the video started, I wish I could have known what I know now. The Buggles weren't just a bunch of alien insects jumping around a weird science lab singing a catchy tune with a great chorus. They were warning us about something that was about to happen. A death in the age of plastic.

"In my mind and in my car
We can't rewind we've gone too far
Video Killed the Radio Star
Video Killed the Radio Star"

People don't get it.

Anyway, I was just sitting there listening to the music as loud as I could handle it and decided to pull out my journals from Ecuador, from my trip there in college. I hadn't read them in a while. I had been planning to share them with Elena at the weekend retreat, but that obviously hadn't worked out.

I opened my journal.

We have been in Duran for a night and a day. We spent a large part of that time sleeping, but we managed to meet a lot of the local people. Last night was spent bathed in sweat and frustration, as it was too hot to get any sleep. I went to the market this afternoon and bought four pineapples and cheese. The walk back up the hill was difficult. There is poverty here such as I have never seen before, but the people don't seem to be depressed or bitter. In fact, they are incredibly high-spirited with an amazing sense of humor, considering the circumstances.

Duran is on a hill overlooking the Guayas River and the city of Guayaquil. It is a beautiful spot dotted with humble shacks and tiny, one-room houses. Tomorrow we go to the interior to visit churches and schools.

It was when a group of us went to the country that the priest who was showing us around Quayaquil, Father Diego, told us a story. As he related his tale, we were in a clearing way out in the countryside, sitting in a circular formation of some rather large rocks.

I will never forget that story.

It seems that in Washington there was a construction worker who had been promoted to the position of area manager for a large construction company. His job was to oversee the company's various building projects in the area. He had spent his life working hard to get where he was, and was now reaping the rewards. He had married a beautiful girl whom he loved madly, and they had two daughters, ages three and five. His workers liked and respected him; he treated them like professionals, never cutting corners to save money on a job, and they, in turn, worked hard for him. Then, on one of those days for which the phrase "bad things happen to good people" was invented, he lost it all. His wife decided to surprise him by taking the girls with her and meeting him for lunch. Three miles from home a recently fired stockbroker, who had been drowning his sorrows at a bar, ran a red light and broadsided her car. He got two broken arms and a punctured lung. The wife and girls were killed instantly. He had everything taken from him, just like that. Everything. Gone. He didn't know who he was or where to turn. It was too much for him to deal with.

He started drinking a bit to numb the pain, then he drank a bit more, than a bit more than that. His fellow workers could imagine what kind of hell he was going through, and they banded together to cover for him when he would stagger into work after a night's binge, or leave several hours early to begin another one. At times he would stumble around the worksite in a daze, at other times he would curl up in a corner and stare into space for hours.

After a few months, even his friends couldn't cover for him anymore. The company president called him in, sat him down and gently told him that, although the company understood his situation and was sorry for his loss, word of his drinking had gotten back to them, and due to the somewhat dangerous nature of his job— performing work at high altitudes, working with industrial electrical wiring, operating heavy construction equipment, etc.—they couldn't allow him to stay on the job in his current condition. They weren't firing him, though; they were going to give him six months off, at full salary, to recover and get his life together, and then he could come back to work at the same position with the same pay.

It was three years later in Seattle when Father Diego met him. Whether he quit or the company fired him, he never said. Even when he wasn't drinking he smelled of beer—which, considering the fact he had been drinking nonstop for the past three years, wasn't all that much of a surprise. Father Diego had a daily mass at 7:30 a.m. attended by a regular group of parishioners. They were mostly older people; the younger ones couldn't find the time. This man, however found the time. At night and into the early morning he would shake and drink and shake and try to make sense of what happened, but when the sun came up there were still no answers. He had no way to get to Mass, so he would call Checker Cab and one of the drivers would take him, come back in an hour, pick him up and take him home. This became a regular occurrence. And, because Father Diego had become aware of this man's tragedy, he never chided him for coming to mass drunk. Drunk people are allowed in church, too. At least, that's what Father Diego thought.

Eventually it was the same driver, Ted, who would pick this man up and take him to church. Ted didn't believe in God. How could he? There was too much suffering in the world, too much pain, too many wars, too many massacres, too much disease, too much greed, too much hatred—and to top it off, the people who made the most noise about how much God loved you were the garishly dressed, badly coiffed television evangelists who spent half their time crying for money. He didn't buy it. But he picked up this guy every morning at seven o'clock. After a while, he didn't wait for the dispatcher to call; he just drove over to the man's house, walked up to the door, opened it, picked him up from the floor or off the kitchen table or from wherever he had passed out, splashed some water in his face, poured some coffee into him and put him in the cab.

This went on for about three months. Ted found himself starting to think of this man as more than just a regular fare and wondered why he was in so much pain. So Ted began going to mass and seeing the way the priests treated this sad, beaten, alcohol-soaked man. He would shake so much that sometimes the priests had to hold his head up so they could put the bread and wine in his mouth for him. Then you could see a change come over him—nothing earth shaking, but a change nonetheless. He would perk up a bit and be able to walk out of the church with only one arm around Ted instead of two.

Three years later Ted entered the priesthood. The man he drove to Mass is still out there somewhere, suffering in his own private hell, trying to numb himself, to make some sense out of the ruins of his life—for his sake, hopefully, not for much longer. In his pain, though, in his drunkenness, in the shards of his shattered life, he still had the strength to show a cynical, world-weary taxi driver the power of the Eucharist and lead him to God.

Anyway. That is the story I have never forgotten and I never will. I try and read that journal from Ecuador every couple of months to remind me of the story. I wish I could find that man and do something for him, give him something of mine that would help him understand why his wife and girls are gone. I don't know what it would be. Every once in a while I picture him meeting with his workers in the morning around the coffee truck, older, smiling, healthy and sober. I hope it comes true.

I turned to another page in my Ecuador journal and turned the music off.

Today I awoke at 6:30 and went to the outdoor market. There were hundreds of people among all the little stands. Everyone was eating and selling chickens and meat and fruits. The smell was nasty.

I saw 50 chickens with broken legs and wings lying in a pile. I also saw a man in a banana truck drinking out of an antifreeze bucket. People were scurrying to and fro, carrying sacks of just about everything. One image that stands out is that of an elderly woman sitting behind a dark, plastic covering in a darkened shack. Her brown eyes somehow lit up the darkness. She reminded me of the Navajos selling turquoise jewelry on the side of the road in Utah.

I wonder where Elena was from in Ecuador and how long she had lived there? What are the chances that when I was trudging up that long hill from the market to Duran I passed her or someone who knew her when she was a little girl? What if her parents were originally from that very town where we, ten idealistic college students, went to learn about the poor and about Liberation Theology and sustainable agriculture and local politics? I wanted to ask her and share with her and connect with her, but I'm beginning to think it's not possible for me to know who she is and where she comes from. Not because I don't want to, but because she seems to have this block. Whenever I get close to her, she pushes me away.

The phone rang.

"Hello."

"Simeon, this is Peter."

"Hey, Peter," I said.

"I went over your dump truck story again and took out the part about the urine and community pool stuff and made it printable. I need that third story as soon as you can get it to me."

"Thanks, Peter. I'll write it now and come into the office."

61

"I'll be here until late, so finish it and then we can go and get something to eat."

"Great," I said, "I'll see you in a few hours." I sat down to write another story. I saved my favorite for last, the one I actually wanted to make into a feature, but Peter didn't think our readers would be interested in it. So I was going to make it short, but sharp. It was a story about the Three Gorges Dam in China and the equipment used in building it.

You will be able to see it from the moon. Over 40,000 people are working on it. Total cost is estimated to be in the vicinity of $75 billion (yes, billion). It will be six times the size of the Hoover Dam in California. There are thousands of cranes, dump trucks and steam shovels working right now. And you can imagine the amount of explosives being used to shape the land. When the dam is completed, over a million people will have been displaced, and 62,000 acres of land will be unde water. It is estimated that this project will take about fifteen years to complete (and you thought that the Euro-Chunnel was a big deal). This thing is huge.

To give you an idea of what is going into this project and what it will look like when it's done: imagine a sixty-story building that is 1.3 miles wide. That's a big dam. But let's not give them credit yet. There is a lot of controversy around the project due to the displacement of so many people and the environmental hazards of the project. There's another thing I've been wondering about the project. Think about this: there are 40,000 people working on this job. Now, cars are expensive in China, and the average Chinese person can't really afford one. He can, however, afford a bicycle. Now of these 40,000 dam employees, I think it's fair to say that the vast majority of them get to work on their bicycles rather than driving their cars, or taking the bus. So you have 40,000 people working three shifts, that's around 13,000 people per shift. Let's say 10,000 of them ride their bikes to work. When they get to work, what do they do with their bikes? Why, park them, of course. Where? Why, in a bike parking lot. Imagine that—a parking lot lined up with 10,000 bikes. What a victory! Imagine the portable showers.

I made my way back to work with my story and walked into the office. I found Peter sitting there alone. Only the light on his desk was on and his computer was reflecting a greenish-blue light on his face.

"Hey, Simeon, you got the story?"

"I do," I said.

"Well, let me read it," said sad Peter.

"Are you all right?" I asked.

"I guess so," he replied, and started looking over the dam story.

He took out the part about the bikes because he was convinced they couldn't ride through all the dirt and mud around the dam. He was probably right, but I wanted to dream a little. It took him twenty minutes to read the story. When he was finished, we headed out to get something to eat.

Peter did seem sad. He was moody. I watched him as we walked downtown and I tried to figure out what was bothering him. Was he mad at me about the Elena thing? Was he mad at something in his life, with the magazine or with someone in his family? Had someone hurt him? Then he spoke, with his hands in his pockets.

"Do you think people are born evil, Simeon, or do you think that society makes them do evil things?" We kept walking.

"I'm not sure," I said. "I wonder the same thing sometimes."

"If you look at all the tragedy in the world, the murders and the infidelity and the corruption and what not, you would think that people are naturally prone to do evil things. I mean, how do you explain the killing fields in Cambodia, the Holocaust, the horrendous slaughters in Rwanda, the genocide in Armenia in the early 1900s? How do people get to a place in their lives where they don't care if they kill—where, in fact, they actually want to kill?"

"I don't know," I said.

"On a smaller scale, how do you explain when someone you love with all your heart, someone you have given your soul and body to, betrays you, cheats on you and leaves you? How does that happen? How does someone who loved you turn so cold and indifferent that they won't even talk to you about how confusing their feelings are and they want some time to sort them out? I realize that people change and love can diminish, and I can handle that. But why do a hurtful, even evil thing when it's better for everyone just to talk about whatever problems there are? Don't they owe you that?"

"They do," I said. "I'm not sure where I stand on the origin of evil or on original sin, especially the evil that escalates into genocide or murder or rape. I don't understand that type of evil. But I do think that people in general are not aware of who they are. Because of that, they get themselves stuck in relationships that eventually go bad and they have to get out. I say that intellectually, but I also know that there is not always a direct line from the intellect to the emotions when it comes to making decisions. How many people do you know who are very successful in work or school, but who date complete losers who take advantage of them and abuse them, emotionally or physically?"

"A few, actually," said Peter.

"I'm not sure, Peter. I'm trying to figure the same thing out in my life right now. I mean, I am falling in love with this Elena girl but I don't know a thing about her. To top it all off, she keeps pleading with me not to get involved with her, but then she tells me that she wants to be with me, then later on she tells me at the retreat that she is with B.D, but I keep pursuing her. I keep thinking about her. I want her. I'm standing here telling you this and giving you advice about the connection between intellect and emotion, and yet, I don't have that connection. The more interesting question for me right now is why do I want her? Of all the people around, I pick one who has a bastard boyfriend, one who left me on our first date, who calls me and invites me on a self-help weekend, kisses me like no other, sleeps in my bed, then rejects me the next morning. Then she calls me down to see her a few days later, tells me I am too good for her and I don't know her, kisses me, then sends me away again. The question shouldn't be how people can be so evil. It's why are we attracted to people like that in the first place?"

"That's true," said Peter.

We kept walking and I began to feel guilty about pouring my guts out to Peter when it was obvious he was the one who needed to talk. I took his microphone away from him by going on and on about my princess and now it didn't look like he had the courage to tell me what was going on in his life. I should have waited to listen to him instead of going on like that. I made a mental note next time to be quiet when a gentle person like Peter was trying to tell me something painful. Note taken.

When I got home that night there was a message from my mom. She was happy and wanted to know how things were going with Elena and work and all. I wanted to call her back but it was getting late, and I was tired of talking. In fact, I felt almost too guilty to talk. I talked too much that night. I grabbed my Greek grammar and started going over some basic declensions until I was too tired to continue. I shut my eyes and asked God to forgive me for not listening better and asked Him to help that man who lost his family and to help gentle Peter to get through his pain. I asked God to help me figure out where to go with Elena, but as I was praying I felt insincere. I wanted help, but I also think I was looking forward to the ride. I wanted intervention, but only if things got so haywire that I would lose my mind.

And things did.

CHAPTER 5

Two weeks had passed since I had made my way to the sweat factory of Pure USA Gym. I hadn't spoken with Elena in all that time, although the phone rang once at around 3:00 a.m. I didn't answer it, though, and the caller didn't leave a message. I was floating around. I think I was waiting for something to happen instead of doing something to make it happen. I didn't really know what my next move was. Peter and I had put to bed another issue of *Man Tractors*, so I had spent two weeks reading and wandering around, thinking about my Xena and her kidnapper and the retreat and what happened and all. I think what I secretly wished was for her to call and profess her love for me. That didn't happen. Peter seemed to be slowly getting better after his breakup, or whatever it was that happened. He never told me the details and I didn't ask.

When I picked up the mail from my box at the mail drop/printing store down the street, there was an envelope from Pure USA Gym. I opened it. It read:

Slowly. Unintentionally. Timidly. Full of fear. You lead your life.

Purposefully. Actively. Energetically. Respectfully. We lead ours.

Want to know more?

Please join us for a talk on how to live your life with purpose and fulfillment. Join us at the Cafe Seville at 7:30 p.m. Wednesday.

Take a wild guess as to who the speaker was going to be. Yes, the famous Menehune descendant himself. The little rodent. The lover of Xena. Why would they think that I would want to go to that talk? The reason I live my life "full of fear" is so that I can stay away from little people like him. I don't know. I walked back home and thought about it for a while and realized that Elena, my dream woman, would most likely be there; if I could steal just one glance from her I would never be hungry again—at least not for a day or two.

I decided to go.

I got to the front of the cafe, an old Victorian building with impressive steps and a blue and white exterior, and walked through the hallowed doors to pay my money for the talk. It was $35 for non-members and $30 for members. I'm glad the $149 they swipe from my credit card every month is finally doing me some good. Out of the corner of my eye I spotted Vic and Kara, my co-conspirators from the self-help weekend. I was dying to know what happened to them after their failed escape.

I walked up to Vic, who had gained considerable weight since the retreat.

"Hi, Simeon," he said, in a voice smooth as butter.

"Hi Vic, hello, Kara. How are you guys doing?"

"Okay," said Vic. "Have you heard about the Men-Being-Men trip?"

"No."

"You should go," said Vic. "Alan and I are."

"Really?" I said. I wasn't sure why Vic would want to go on another trip with these people.

"Hey, there's B.D.," said Vic. "Why don't you ask him about it?"

"Okay," I said.

The little dictator walked over to me with a strange look on his face. He seemed disappointed in me.

"Hi, Simeon," he ventured.

"Hi, B.D," I said timidly.

He asked me if I could come talk to him for a minute in the other room before the lecture began. I agreed and followed him. Why I did that I don't know. What was I doing back with this group of people again? Then the famous Menehune descendant spoke.

"Simeon, I was a little disappointed that you left the Jump Retreat without talking to me or any of the other leaders. I wanted to find out what happened and make amends with you."

"Well," I said, "I just wanted to leave. The whole thing was a little too much for me at the time and I didn't want to take part in the Fruit Salad workshop." I didn't, of course, tell him his girlfriend spent the night in my room, in my arms, and that I had fled the weekend in

69

fear and confusion. Also, I neglected to tell him I was ferried away in a pink Thunderbird by my boss, Peter.

"I understand, Simeon. Well, I didn't want to get off on the wrong foot with you because Elena tells me you are an interesting and kind person. Shall we start over?" he asked.

"Sure," I said.

"Good. I'm sure you have heard about the Men-Being-Men weekend coming up. I would be honored if you would join us." Then he turned to leave.

"I'll think about it," I said.

I walked back and took a seat next to Vic and Kara and waited for the lecture to begin. It did, only I wasn't listening. I was dreaming about Elena and her eyes and her history and the way she kissed me. While the short one was prattling on about fear and self-realization and letting go of the past, I was strolling shirtless on South American beaches, hand-in-hand with my Latina princess. Then we would stop off at one of those exotic bars that magically appear on these beaches and have a beer and a snack, our legs entwined and our hands together. Then we would head back to our jungle room to take a nap and remain in bed until late in the evening, when we would shower and head to dinner in a warm tropical breeze under the stars. She wore things that were shockingly colorful and soft. And they were different every day.

"Well, thank you for coming," said B.D., "and please don't forget to sign up for the two trips coming up in two weeks. Visualize yourself as something more than you really are. Good night," he said.

Great. I had just paid $30 to have an hour-long fantasy vacation with Elena in some unknown place.

It was a nice place, though. I hope it really exists. I made my way to the back of the room to avoid any more contact with the group, grabbed a flyer about the Men-Being-Men trip and headed out the door. I went home and pretended I was at that bar again and then fell asleep.

When I got to work the next morning Peter looked sad again. I reminded myself that the last time he looked this way I selfishly stole his thunder and droned on about my own problems. Today, I decided I was going to listen.

"Hey, sunshine," I said, patting his back. "Why do you look so sad?"

"Do you have a minute?" he asked gently.

"Sure do."

We sat down in that room where we spent so much time together, talking and writing about the things that mattered to us, things our readers would want to know about. Now Peter was about to talk about something that mattered to him but that our readers would not only not want to read, but wouldn't even want to know about. Peter looked at me sadly and began to tell me a story about his nephew.

It turns out his nephew Andrew was one of those extremely bright and sensitive kids. Comfortable with his family and friends he was self-confident and amiable, but, out in public, among people he didn't know, he was visibly distant. Andrew was really interested in space and rockets, and so he began to build and paint rockets in his garage

71

after school. Then, once a month, he and his mom would go out to the desert with fellow rocket aficionados and launch them. Andrew really enjoyed this, but Peter said he started to become obsessed with the whole concept of rockets and space and launches. It was all he could think about.

For two years he would spend all his waking hours in the garage building elaborate and expensive rockets instead of going out to movies or dances or any of the things kids his age do. His mom knew how much he loved rockets, and, considering what most kids were into, she supported him. In fact, she took on a job two nights a week to pay for his expensive hobby. After a while she began to notice a change, though. Instead of going to the rocket launches and talking with people and getting ideas and enjoying the community aspect of the group, he would concentrate on his own rocket to the exclusion of anyone and anything else. For days before the event he would check and double check and triple check everything. On the day of the launch, he would talk to no one.

His mom began to worry and finally got up the nerve to ask him why he was acting so intensely, and wasn't it just all for fun anyway and that sort of stuff. He didn't respond. In fact, he stopped responding to anything, and, a month ago, his mother had finally committed him to a psychiatric home outside of Napa Valley, California. He was diagnosed as severely depressed and delusional.

Peter's sister told him the doctors found out he had been writing letters up to twenty pages long, single-spaced, and stuffing them into his rockets. He was convinced that when the rocket finally exploded, the letters would somehow manage to get to the person for whom they were intended. Andrew was writing letters to God and sending them up into the heavens to make sure that God got them. The letters were about war and poverty and hatred and disease and divorce and abuse and a lot of other questions most people have but are afraid to ask God. He was intensely curious. He was going to stay at the funny farm for the summer and then, after promising to refrain from rocket launching while being heavily medicated, he would be released.

Peter was going to take him in for a while because his sister was not dealing with the situation well at all, and they both felt Andrew would feel better with some stability around him. He was going to come to work with us and Peter wanted to know what I thought and if I would mind. I told him I would not mind at all; in fact, I looked forward to getting to know him. Peter spun his chair around and went back to writing, or editing, or just staring at the computer. I wanted to tell him all about the meeting and about the Men-Being-Men trip and get his opinion, but I let this day be about him and his nephew and I begrudgingly sat there, made some phone calls and didn't mention anything about me or the trip.

After going over and over it in my head for the next few days, I finally decided to go. Why not? I had nothing else going on in my life and it sounded sort of fun; maybe this B.D. guy wasn't all that bad. Elena liked him. In fact, Elena seemed to love him, which actually was a minor problem. So, I decided to join Vic and Alan and B.D. and go on the Men-Being-Men trip. I didn't tell Peter what I was doing. In fact, I fibbed and told him I was going back to North

73

Dakota to visit my mom for a few days. In truth, I was heading to Oregon for a four-day river-rafting, vision-quest adventure complete with yoga, tai-chi, war painting, drum making and a bunch of other guy kinds of stuff.

Wednesday came faster than I had anticipated. We were putting together a comprehensive buyer's guide of tractors for the next issue, so I didn't have to write any major stories, just a list of tractors and their specifications and prices. It was pretty simple. Peter was detached because he was thinking about Andrew and getting his extra room ready and about being a stable influence on his nephew. I slipped out that Wednesday and made my way down to the gym to meet up with the rest of the men. They were all there waiting, wearing green sweatshirts that read,

MEN BEING MEN

VISION QUEST

ROGUE RIVER, OREGON

B.D. handed me a sweatshirt and I said hello to Vic and Alan and Fred. Fred was the vision quest leader complete with credentials from the School of Lost Borders, the Dance of the Elk Foundation and the International Center for the Dances of Universal Peace, or so I found out later. We loaded up the van and headed to Santa Barbara's small airport to catch a plane that would fly us to San Francisco. We would fly from there to Medford and take a van to our camp outside of Grants Pass. I looked at a map on the second leg of our flight and noticed how close Ashland was to Grants Pass, and I wished that we were going to the Shakespeare Festival there instead of a river rafting, vision-quest man trip. I think it was mostly nerves, though. As it turned out, I was nervous for good reason.

When we finally got to our camp near Grants Pass we were instructed by Fred to put away our gear and come to the table where we would talk about the next four days. We all sat down and I watched Fred as he fumbled through his folder and took out three envelopes that had each one of our names on it. He told us that he and B.D. were the leaders of the trip and they had done this four or five times before and there was nothing to be nervous about. He told us three was the perfect number of participants because the trip was really about personal solo questing, not group therapy. He told us he was trained as an ecotherapist, a psychodramatist, vision-quest leader and breathing instructor. B.D. then stood up and told us he was trained in solo questing, yoga instruction, tai-chi, face-painting and drum circles. I think he made the painting and drum thing up, but who knows? The guy has some strange talents. And he performs them with quite a tan.

We opened up our envelopes as instructed by Fred and found Native American names typed on the paper. Alan's read Wandering Bull, Vic's Big Brown Bear and mine was Wounded Wolf. I wanted to change my name. I liked Vic's name better. Fred told us we would find out the significance of the names sometime during the quest and not to worry. We had to start calling people by their new names immediately. Fred and B.D. were simply Shaman One and Shaman

Two, respectively. Then we had some dinner sitting around the campground. All vegetarian. The whole weekend was to be vegetarian, according to Wandering Bull, who had been on a few of these things already. Big Brown Bear told me that one of the reasons he and Kara had decided to go on these trips was to lose some weight.

"Why did you decide to come, Wounded Wolf?" asked Wandering Bull.

"I'm not sure, Big Bull," I said.

"It's Wandering Bull," said Alan.

"Sorry, Wandering Bull," I said.

Big Brown Bear told us that Kara and Elena had gone on a trip called "Her Wild Music" to the Joshua Tree State Park outside of Palm Springs. We would find out more about that later.

We made our way to our tents and Shaman One told us to get a good night's rest and he would wake us up in the morning for our first day of preparation. We were to have one day of preparation, one day of solo questing, and then one day of re-entry. I got in my sleeping bag and wondered if Shaman Two, the little bastard, was going to call Elena over the weekend and tell her he loved her. I loved her, but I didn't know why. Maybe being Wounded Wolf for four days would help me figure that out. It couldn't hurt. As I closed my eyes I thought about what was going on. I had paid $1700 to go on a four-day vision quest led by two freaks in Southern Oregon. We were going to river raft, breathe in circles, paint ourselves, fast, do yoga, solo quest and who knows what else. I was beginning to feel uncomfortable with my decision. Wandering Bull began to snore. I threw a pair of my socks at him and he stopped. The poor guy. I wondered how much money he had spent on these weekends. He couldn't help it. And, it seems, neither could Big Brown Bear and I. And then I fell asleep.

It wasn't long before Shaman One and Two woke me up by shaking my sleeping bag violently.

"Are you ready for your preparation, Wounded Wolf?"

"Right now?" I responded.

"Get up," they said.

And I did. They walked me, half asleep, down to the Rogue River and told me to jump in the water.

"Right now?" I asked.

"Yes, Wounded Wolf, now," said Shaman Two.

Shaman One went with me and told me to hold my breath and when I wanted to come up for air to tap his arm, which would be holding my head under water. The water was so cold. What the hell was I doing? I was in all my clothes. Do these guys have major problems or what? I went underwater, half asleep, confused, trying to hold my breath for as long as I possibly could. I lasted for maybe ten seconds, and I tapped on Shaman One's arm, but he didn't pull me up; he pushed me back down. I was panicking. I began shaking my legs and trying to break free, but he kept pushing down. Five seconds went by and he pulled me up and I jumped out of the water and tried to tackle him while coughing and gasping for air. Then I turned around and saw Wandering Bull, Big Brown Bear and Shaman Two standing on the shore, applauding me. Shaman One hugged me and said he was sorry but that I had just been through my preparation. They had woken up the other two campers earlier and done the same thing. It was a staged, near-drowning experience that was supposed to make us want to fight to stay alive. That fight was our inner-light, our life-force. And in order to know we had it, we had to feel it. I came out swinging, which meant that I wanted to live. It meant I had purpose and determination and spunk.

"You have the life-force, Wounded Wolf," said Shaman One, "and you have it bad."

I stopped being mad at him and felt, oddly, good. I was cold and shaken up, but it made me feel better that they had tried to drown the other two campers as well. Big Brown Bear had tears in his eyes and he walked me back up to camp with his arm around me.

Once we dried off, we sat down to have some strange breakfast that consisted of lots of roots and nuts and berries but no bacon or ham or sustaining food. I was cold. Wandering Bull looked detached and frustrated and Big Brown Bear had nuts stuck in his teeth. There we were having this bizarre breakfast at the head of the Rogue River, three men and two Shamans. I couldn't wait to tell Peter about this. But I would wait until it was my turn to talk. I started thinking about his nephew and about his letters to God and the rockets and all. When I came home from this freak weekend he would probably be coming in to the office to work with us. I was looking forward to that.

Then Fred stood up from all the nuts and said, "Today is your day of preparation. You will eat plenty of sustainable food today, for tomorrow all you will have on your solo quest is water. Today is the day you prepare your mind and body for a physical and emotional journey. We will soon get on our raft and start down the river. At that point there will be complete silence on the boat. Shaman Two and I are experienced rafters so you do not need to worry. We will be traveling about three miles down the river to make our first camp. We will stop and have lunch and then work on some breathing techniques to get our minds and souls ready for the quest. Are there any questions?"

Big Brown Bear raised his hand.

"Yes, I would like to call my wife Kara before the silence begins to tell her that I love her."

"I will take care of that for you, Big Brown Bear," said Shaman Two. "I will be talking to the leaders of the Her Wild Song weekend periodically and I will make sure that Kara knows you are thinking about her."

"All right," said the Bear, timidly.

That smug Shaman Two. Can't the poor guy talk to his wife? I was beginning to regret this weekend; the silence, the food—or lack of it; the river, the drowning exercise. I was cold. I grabbed another unsalted nut and chewed on it. I wanted a cigarette or some form of tobacco. Didn't the Native Americans chew tobacco or smoke or something? I decided to ask.

"Shaman One, didn't the Native Americans chew tobacco or smoke or something?"

"Yes, they did," he said.

"Well, do you think we could do that as well? You know, in order to understand our names and their significance a little better?"

"No," said Shaman Two. "The point of this weekend is to rid yourselves of poisons and things that are getting in your way. I thought you quit smoking anyway, Wounded Wolf."

"I did. But I thought this weekend would be a good time to start up again, what with being outdoors and almost drowning and all."

They, meaning the Shaman partners, just smiled as if I was a weak rat. Then, like the curtains coming down after a boring musical, Fred lowered the shroud of silence on us as we grabbed our stuff and headed to the yellow and red raft.

"We will refrain from speaking now," he said. We walked to the boat, shivering and scared.

CHAPTER 6

Wandering Bull and I sat in front and Big Brown Bear, due in part to his girth, sat in the middle to stabilize the raft. We weren't allowed to talk, so I began to look around at the trees and the birds and listen to the water splash and daydream. My thoughts started out as normal thoughts: work, Peter, Andrew, my mom, my weight, my hunger, my desire for tobacco, my love of wine, the Egyptians and their pyramids and their cat and dog gods, sport utility vehicles, the white faces and bodies of people that live in cities like New York, subways, policemen, guns, war, tornadoes, large birds and then flashes of candy bars and cows and steak and pork and ham and bologna and cheese and Italy and the Romans and the Greeks and Sappho and her lesbian pals and things like that.

Then I started to really daydream. There I was at the front of one of the ships called to the Trojan War to help my fellow Greeks destroy the Trojans and seize the harlot Helen and return her to her husband. Only it wasn't Helen of Troy I was fighting for. It was

Elena of Ecuador. The ships weren't long and ancient and Greek; they were shaped like 1967 Chevy Novas and were lowered with big windows and music was pumping and I had black hair and my jeans were sagging around the beginning of my tailbone and I wore lots of jewelry. People were calling me names that I had tattooed all over my chest and back. The area of town where my parents lived was tattooed on both arms as a gift to my parents for choosing such a great house to live in.

There I was, floating to sea, with the rest of my neighborhood in similar low-rider ships, heading off to get Elena. She was stolen, living in a palace, and we were heading to a battle that would take ten years and one in which great heroes would die; history and civilizations for thousands of years would be talking about it. I pulled up my pants, but not too far. I looked back at the angry sea and stared it in the eye, challenging it to take on my Nova. A ship that was owned by a middle- class white couple fifteen years ago.

Wandering Bull tapped my arm and pointed to a clean, sandy beach. The Shamans headed the barge toward it. I had seen this beach before; it was Troy, and it was where we would spend the next few years, playing music and listening to poets and making plans to destroy the city and rescue my Elena and … wait, wait, this wasn't Troy, it was a rocky riverbank outside Grants Pass, Oregon, where I was spending a vision-quest weekend with two other poor saps, and the whole thing was costing me almost two grand. Where did I get the idea I was erecting a siege camp on the plains outside fabled

Troy? Maybe there was something in those nuts they insisted on feeding us. I don't know.

I do know that I was hungry after our journey down the Rogue and I was hoping we were going to be served something a bit more substantial than roots and berries. Maybe a fisherman had buried a pack of cigarettes in the sand just in case a tractor journalist on a man's vision-quest weekend would come upon them in a time of great need. I surveyed the plains of Troy. No such luck, but I would persevere. We unpacked our stuff and set up two tents, one for three regular Native Americans, and one for the blessed Shaman partners. I bet they had Spam in their tent and beer and were smoking French cigarettes at night while plotting to drown us. Bastards. We got all our stuff together and were motioned to follow the leader inland a bit to a rocky area about 200 yards from the beach. We sat down on the rocks and listened to Fred breathe in circles.

I began to watch Fred with a mind full of anger. Here was this man who, to the naked eye, was just another faceless drone walking down the street, but this weekend he had become something much more. He was a Shaman. He continued to breathe in circles and was flapping his arms gracefully up and down and around, staring at us like we should do the same. He looked like a big duck. There he was flapping away, standing on a rock, and it became apparent to me that he was slowly beginning to believe he was really a Native American priest, flapping and breathing. I tried the breathing. I inhaled deeply, held it in my lungs for a few seconds, then expelled it. I was starting to get dizzy. No wonder people who only eat vegan, or whatever they call it, are always sort of spaced out. They don't get enough nutrients and then they breathe like this. How do they function at a baseball game? They probably don't go, too patriarchal, or macho, or something. This Fred was obviously an interesting bird. I came to find out later, after the quest, that he had, at one time, sold Porsches in Newport Beach and drove a little red model 911 with license plates that read "Inlitend1," and a bumper sticker that said, "Goddess on Board." Go figure. Anyway, I continued breathing and now Wandering Bull and Big Brown Bear were standing up and flapping their arms like ducks, so I stood up.

I kept breathing and flapping. Then, like a duck landing on a fake lake in Palm Springs, he sat down and crossed his legs in a yoga-like position and began to hum loudly. The bear and the bull sat down and followed, as did I. Only I didn't hum. I was waiting to hear the others first. The bull began, probably because he had done this sort of thing before, and then the bear started in. Shaman One never looked up so I decided I wasn't going to make a sound and I was going to sit there and see if anyone noticed. Hmmm.

It continued and I made the first of many rebellious moves by standing up and stretching and speaking out loud,

"Shaman One. This is Wounded Wolf. I need something to eat or I might die." He just shook his head and motioned with his index finger up to his lips and then fanned both his hands up and down as if to let me know I should sit back down. And I did.

A few minutes later, Shaman Two, the famous Menehune fitness freak, walked up to the rocks and motioned me to come over to him. I was in trouble already and it was only the second day. I followed him and watched his miniature frame mold and twist and conform to all the bumps and minor elevation changes on the way back down to the beach. We sat down by the two tents.

"Now, Wounded Wolf, I am breaking the silence because I think it will help you in your preparation. It has become obvious to Shaman Two and me that you are struggling with this weekend, while the other two are doing just fine. I don't want you to speak but I want you to write in the sand when I speak the truth of your situation."

I nodded.

"Are you regretting that you came here?"

I wrote, "A little bit."

"Are you scared for your well-being?"

I put a check mark by my first statement.

"Are you hungry?"

I wrote, "Yes!"

"Do you want to get something out of this weekend?"

I put a check mark by my second statement.

"Well, then, Wounded Wolf, I think you are doing just fine, but your life force is rebelling against all of this. It could just mean that you are strong and stubborn and in the end you could end up making more progress than any of us. I have a feeling, Wounded Wolf, that the next two days are going to do wonders for you. I believe in you. Now, believe in yourself and trust in your light and you will be more than fine."

I looked into his eyes and was convinced he meant what he said. He did. And I was so hungry and confused he could have told me that in two hours I was going to lead the United States into war against alien soldiers on the moon and I would have believed him. The bull and the bear came walking up and Shaman Two followed, putting his hands together and placing them on his cheek to indicate that it was time for us to get some rest before dinner. It had been a long day already and it was only around 3:00 p.m. He motioned his finger to his lip and went into his tent with the tanned one. At this point I considered writing in the sand that I had been diagnosed as a mild hypoglycemic as a child and that it was imperative I get more to eat, but I didn't have the energy. My blood sugar level was way too low. I felt dizzy and went in the tent and sat down.

I slept, but the thought of being pulled out of bed for another near-drowning experience hovered around my mind. When I opened my eyes I noticed the bear and the bull were still asleep. Probably all the humming tired them out. I looked at Big Brown Bear and he looked a shade of orange because the sun was coming through the material of the tent and I thought about how much money he and Kara had spent on this weekend and I sincerely hoped it would do him and them some good.

I closed my eyes again for what seemed like a minute when I was woken up by the sound of drums outside the tent. The three of us looked at each other and made our way outside to find Shaman One and Shaman Two in the Half-Lotus position, completely naked, banging on drums and motioning us to take off our clothes and assume the Half-Lotus on the beach. They had red and yellow war paint on their faces. East meets West.

This was about all I could take. I started to laugh and I laughed so hard I keeled over and fell onto the sand. I looked over to the bull to see if he thought it was funny as well, but he was taking off his pants and underwear and moving to the beat. And, to my dismay, so was the Big Brown Bear. Naked. Shaman One put his index finger up to his lips and looked at me with a certain amount of compassion. They beat on. I stood there for a moment in suspended disbelief.

Then, in a show of complete submission and desperation, I undressed. I began with my shirt and then my shoes, and, slowly but surely, I was naked on the beach with the bull and the bear in the Half-Lotus position. And the drums were being beaten. The Half-Lotus position is not that difficult with clothes on, but due to certain realities of the male physique it was quite a task to fold my legs into my inner thighs. The bear wasn't even close to the position but what he lacked in execution he made up for in intensity. The bull did fine. We remained in this position on the beach in the nude for a few minutes until Shaman Two put his drum down and walked toward us and displayed a white piece of construction paper that read,

Position Two: The Pose of A Frog

He assumed the pose. He sat with his knees wide apart, toes together, his hands raised and his palms together over his head. This was an interesting position to find yourself in while naked. The bear

87

wasn't even close. He got the hands over the head part correct but that was about it. While we were in this position, Shaman Two walked over to each of us and rubbed war paint on our faces and the other healer continued to beat the drums. I wish I could have seen myself but instead I just watched the bull. Red and yellow streaks going down his face. Shaman Two broke the silence.

"I will speak quietly to explain the different positions to you as they will help you in preparation for your quest. The Pose of a Frog is designed to strengthen your knees and instep and to stimulate your abdominal organs and aid in your digestion. This position also tones up and purifies your genital organs." He took a deep breath and let it out as if he was demonstrating the claim he just made.

Great. That's just what I need—genital toning and purification. I bet the tanned bastard does this position a lot. I was trying to remain positive, though, so I watched and breathed in and out and finally came to the conclusion that a little toning couldn't hurt. The bear was struggling.

After a few more minutes of drumming and the frog position, the bastard held up another card that read,

Position Three: Pose of a Lion

He assumed the next position and we all struggled to follow. He put his legs together and sat back on his heels, put his hands on his knees, with his back straight, opened his mouth, put his tongue out as far as it would go and tilted it out toward the sun. He held the position for a minute so we could see what he was doing and then spoke gently.

"This position strengthens the throat and the root of the tongue. Make sure the sun can get down inside your throat and fuel your life force." This was a tough position, with our tongues hanging out and all. We held it for a few seconds, then released and did it again. The bear wasn't doing so hot. He had a tiny tongue for a bear his size, and every time he would tilt his head to let the sun down his throat he would lose his balance and fall over. The poor guy. The drums kept beating. For a moment while I had my tongue as far out as it would go and my head tilted to let the sun get to know my life force I thought about potential campers across the river and how, if they just happened to float on by while we were sitting there naked, painted and with our tongues out, they might never recover. I don't blame them.

After a few more minutes in that position, Shaman Two held up another card:

Position Four: The Dangerous Pose

He assumed the position with his thighs crossed so they overlapped and his right foot was on the left side of the body and the left foot by the right side. This was a tough one. Then he put his hands with fingers extended and palms down on the uppermost knee. And he breathed. And we tried. The bear was falling over and looked frustrated. And then the healer explained the position.

89

"This pose, while difficult, is very important. It is used by the celibate yogis to transmute sexual energy into physical or mental energy."

Oh, great. We were naked. Things were not working. I could see the bear was having trouble with the Dangerous Pose. He was trying to force his legs into the position and, like a flash of thunder and lightning, the Big Brown Bear went down.

"Oh no, my cojones, my cojones!"

He was rolling on the ground naked, smeared with war paint, which seemed to me an odd time to be screaming in two different languages. Just then a boat drifted by with three men who were standing up with fishing poles and I heard one of them ask, "What in the hell is going on over there?"

I pretty much froze right then and there in the Dangerous Pose. No wonder they called it that. I was so confused and nude and all painted up and everything. Shaman One and Two were standing over Big Brown Bear all painted up and nude and all. It was a complete scene. I saw the three fishermen in the normal boat paddling away as fast as they could, shaking their heads in concentrated retreat. I wonder what they were thinking. I know what I was thinking: Poor bear. I walked over to see if I could help at all and the healers waved me off as they rubbed his shoulders and began to paint his arms with more paint and tell him he was a strong bear and a big bear and he was going to be all right. If his wife could see him now. Somehow I thought that this would not turn her on, and, if it did, then their relationship had more problems than a man weekend could address.

I walked over to Wandering Bull and broke the silence.

"Do you think he's all right, Alan?"

He didn't respond.

"Alan … do you think Vic is all right?"

He just looked at me with his face painted, all naked, and put his index finger to his lips and began to write something in the sand. I was amazed he wouldn't talk to me. It took him a while to write it out and it said, "My name is Wandering Bull."

"C'mon, Alan, it's me, Simeon. Can you please wake up and talk to me like a human? This whole name thing and the paint and the nakedness is a little much, don't you think?"

He just shook his head and looked out into the distance like a young Apache contemplating his first trip into battle with a neighboring tribe.

Then Big Brown Bear got up with the help of the healers and began walking over to the tent.

"He's going to be all right," they said. "He just needs to rest." They motioned the bull and I over to the fire pit and gestured for us to sit down.

We sat there, the brainwashed bull and I, in silence, catching our breath and watching the healers take the big bear into their tent and lay him down to rest. It was at this point I think I realized how stupid this whole weekend was. I mean, what if the bear had incurred some permanent injury to his cojones; what would Kara say? How was I going to explain this to Peter? They all stayed in there awhile, and I heard one of them talking on a cellular phone. Then, the two Shamans walked over to us and Shaman One spoke.

"I am breaking the silence to explain to you two what happened, so you can both continue on with your quest. Big Brown Bear is down for the count. He has pulled his groin muscle; in fact, we think he might have torn it. We have called the Rogue River Rescue Unit and they are bringing a boat down here and then are going to airlift the bear to Grants Pass where he can get some medical attention. This stuff happens during quests. Some people just aren't cut out for it. We think it is imperative, however, that you two continue without Big Brown Bear. Now, if you will head to your tent in silence, Shaman Two and I will wait for the rescue unit and then we can all proceed."

Poor bear. I wonder what he is going to tell the rescue personnel when they arrive. I doubt he is going to tell them what really happened: "Well, we were all painted up and doing nude yoga when my cojones sustained a permanent injury. In fact, it happened two positions after the Frog Pose in which my genitals were being purified. Maybe I overdid it," Vic would say. I don't know. I hope they put some clothes on him and take the war paint off his body, so at least he can hold onto what is left of his dignity, torn groin and all. The brainwashed bull and I sat in our tents and started writing in our quest journals as instructed.

CHAPTER 7

This is what I wrote:

Well, what should I say?   This is our second day and we have already lost one person, Vic, or Big Brown Buddy, or whatever the hell his name is. I am unhappy. They tried to drown me this morning and my college buddy won't speak with me and will only respond by writing in the sand when I address him as Wandering Bull. I feel like crying. I haven't forgiven my father yet and I don't feel more manly. I have not tapped into my life force, although the two shamans insist that I have one. Maybe I should tell them my life force is on hiatus and doesn't want to come out right now. Who knew? I feel sick to my stomach that I spent so much money on this trip. I could have bought a new computer or a new car or at least something tangible.

I'm thinking a lot right now, which I guess is a good thing. I'm nude. I have war paint all over my face and I am sweating in this tent.   Wandering Bull is sitting over there writing furiously in his journal, probably about his parents and how they don't love him much and how he had a tendency to steal alcohol while catering. I am extremely anxious as I hear the boat coming up to our beach. I hope to God that the two freaks don't walk out to the rescuers in their native garb. What will they think? They will probably call the sheriff and have us all carted away to a mental facility, which is probably not a bad thing. At least my insurance would cover the cost.

93

Brad Roe

Why do I get myself in these situations? I am trying to concentrate and at least get something out of it, but it is so odd. I am trying to get better or get with it or get something, but I can't help but be cynical. I am breathing heavy. I know we have a lot ahead of us on this weekend and I am scared to be left here with these freaks for the next two days. Tomorrow begins my solo quest. I don't get to eat and I have to sit in one spot under a tree and wait for enlightenment. I hope it comes my way early in the day and then I will run through the forest and try to find some campers and plead with them to get me out of here. That is my plan as of now.

I put my head down on the pillow and tried to close my eyes and think about something nice. I ended up thinking about that beach bar again in South America. This time I ordered some appetizers with my beer and Elena was in the rest room freshening up. I ate the appetizers while she was gone and ordered another one before she returned. When she finally did return her hair was wet and she smelled of gardenias and rose oil. Her hands were dark brown and glistening as she took a sip of cold beer. I lit up a smoke and inhaled the tobacco and her scent all at once, and then exhaled to the side while watching her smile with love and infatuation. All for me. I wanted to buy the bar and sit there forever, but instead I was in a tent—and in the tent I would remain while the two healers delivered the injured bull to the authorities. I fell asleep thinking about my mom and her home for kids and how I should probably go work for her someday and get to know Father Michael and all. But for now, I am on the beach in Troy, waiting for the battle, thinking about Elena of Ecuador.

I remained in the tent with Wandering Bull, trying to sleep, and I think I was asleep when my dad once again popped into my head. I think one of the reasons he doesn't care about what is going on in my life is that his life is riddled with lawsuits. I heard from my mom that a few years back he and another doctor from optometry school began a new surgical procedure to try to correct nearsightedness or, as they call it, myopia. The procedure began in the Soviet Union and is called Radial Keratotomy. It sounds confusing but it really isn't.

Myopia causes blurred vision of distant objects and affects about twenty-percent of the human population, probably some animals too, but that is another story. So, distant images can become blurred. Most distant images become blurred unless you are like my dad. I bet he is able to spot the marquees of strip joints a mile away while whizzing by at seventy miles an hour. He has selective myopia.

Anyway, they began the experimental surgery in a small town outside Seattle called Spath. Their clinic performed the surgery on almost 2000 people over a three-year period, before it was covered by insurance and deemed legitimate by a large group of eye doctors. People came from all over the world to get the expensive surgery. The surgery consists of small incisions in the cornea made in a radial pattern. If everything goes well the center of the cornea flattens out and changes the way the light rays are bent. Something like that. Half of the patients ended up with perfect eyesight and my dad was the talk of the town. He was on television and interviewed in papers and medical journals.

About 100 people, however, experienced major complications. If the incisions are a fraction of a millimeter off, strange things can happen that even eyeglasses are unable to fix. Almost all of the affected patients began seeing visions of pink elephants dancing or spinning uncontrollably in a circle. It was dubbed by my dad and his Russian counterpart The Pink Elephant Syndrome. You can imagine the uproar. These poor people would be driving or playing golf or at the ball game when, if the light entered their eyes in a certain way, pink elephants began to appear, dancing away. A few of the patients went wacko and had to be admitted to one of those places where Peter's nephew spent some time.

My dad and his now mad Russian counterpart had to close down their clinic in Spath and head for the hills. Since the procedure was experimental, the lawsuits weren't covered under their malpractice insurance policy. He again became the talk of the town, but not for the same reasons as before. Half of the people suffering from the Pink Elephant Syndrome got together and slapped a lawsuit against my dad and Dr. Yureg. The Russian fled to Argentina and began working on large farm animals that didn't complain about much and didn't have lawyers. My dad, on the other hand, was forced to move from state to state trying to work, but usually losing his job when the Pink Elephant stories caught up with him. He had already lost all his money, so the only recourse these people had was to make sure he never worked again. Maybe that is why he likes beer and women so much. It gets him away from the elephants and the people who see them dancing at baseball games.

I had started to feel sorry for him for a moment when my daydream was put to an end by Shaman One motioning us to come outside of the tent. We followed and Shaman One spoke:

"We lost the bear, but we didn't lose you. He is going to be all right. Tonight is the last step of your preparation before you began your solo quest in the morning. It is essential that you both refrain from speaking for the next few hours. We are going to eat some nuts and berries and sit by the fire in the Lotus Position and we want you to think about your life from your first memories as a child to the present. This might be challenging and painful but it will prepare your soul for tomorrow. We will go to bed early so you can rest up for tomorrow. I send you my light so that you will be able to see your soul clearly."

I wanted to say, "Hey, thanks for the light" but I didn't. The talking thing wasn't going to be a problem, since Wandering Bull was so brainwashed by this whole thing that I was convinced he would never speak again. At least, not to me. I thought about all the money I had spent on this weekend and tried to relax and concentrate on my life a little. There was nothing else to do, and, at least now, we had clothes on.

I focused on the firepot and noticed the three other campers had their eyes closed. It had been a long day, and I didn't have the energy to think about my childhood. I took my soul and my body and went to bed, alone, without the snoring of Wandering Bull.

I slept well but was nervous about the next day, so I woke up every few hours and looked outside the tent to see what was going on.

Sometime in the morning the healers were going to come into the tent, wake us up and send us into the forest with water and our journals, where we would remain for the entire day and into the night. It was the climax of the weekend. It was our quest. I was ready for it, but a little nervous. I think I knew in the back of my mind that when it was over, we would be able to go home, so my attitude was pretty good. At least, for a little while.

When morning came we were awakened by the two pseudo-Native Americans wearing native costumes and beating drums. Wandering Bull and I got out of bed, passively allowed the healers to put war paint all over our bodies and strap on a diaper-like short made of deerhide. They gave us moccasins to wear and three bald eagle feathers. Shaman One spoke.

"Today will be the most important day of your life. You are going to be alone with the Creator. You will not be hindered by food or chemicals. You will have only water to nourish your soul and body. You will go places your soul has never been. It is essential that you don't move from your chosen area. You will remain under a sacred tree all day and into the night. At the end of your quest, Shaman Two and I will come for you and take you back to camp for your period of re-entry. Don't be afraid. Although you will not be able to see us, we will be watching you. Grab your journals and when you feel the need to talk or walk, just write about it. You will now be blindfolded. I am sending you our light and the light of the world to guide your soul on the journey. Our souls will be with you on your journey. Good luck, Wandering Bull, and good luck, Wounded Wolf."

They blindfolded us with something that felt like pantyhose. For a moment I had this sinking feeling Elena had donated them and it was all some sick joke that I had to wear them around my eyes on the way to an 18-hour solo quest without any food or entertainment. They had walked us for what seemed like an hour when I noticed I was only hearing one other set of steps, which meant Wandering Bull was being taken to a different location so we didn't talk or throw rocks at each other or something. I wouldn't mind throwing a rock at him to wake him up a bit. He probably had vodka hidden somewhere in his deer-hide diapers. The bastard. I was getting tired.

Finally, I felt Shaman One stop and lead me down to the ground and he told me to sit in the Lotus position. He asked me to count to 199 and to take the blindfold off at that point. He put his hands on my head and held them there until I got to twenty, then he left. I guess the Newport Beach Porsche salesman was blessing me with all the light of Orange County and south to San Diego. That is a lot of light. I wasn't feeling illuminated, however. When I got to 100 I turned around and looked but there was nobody there. I was at the base of a large pine tree. There was already sap on my back and a little on my deer-hide diaper. I couldn't stop thinking that I was going to remain there for over 18 hours. I thought about ways to pass the time and began collecting little rocks and pine needles and doing my best to put them in a pile out of which I quickly planned to build a small mall with outlets of all the major stores and a large, jumbo Honey Baked

Ham store that offered large, free samples. I was already hungry. The mall didn't get very far; it was abandoned in the planning stages when I realized there was a large colony of ants nearby that was interested in my arrival. I began to throw dirt and small rocks in their direction to let them know, instantly, that I was in town and I was going to need some space. They seemed to cooperate.

I wasn't feeling any light. My inner force had not spoken yet. But, to be fair, I had only been questing for about ten minutes. Maybe this sort of thing takes a little time. Then I came up with an idea: If I exercise a lot, I will get tired and hungry and maybe be able to fall asleep for a few hours to kill some time. I began to run in place and jump up and down. I thought to myself while breathing heavily. I am sitting in the middle of a forest in Oregon with my face painted, wearing a deer-hide diaper. Now I am running in place and jumping up and down. I have reached an all-time low. It is obvious I am going to need some professional help. I pictured my mom and Father Michael watching me from a distance and my dad, who was probably used to this sort of thing but who actually thought I was a band of pink elephants dancing in a circle. And Elena. She would be proud of me, I think, jumping up and down here in the forest. Who knows what she would think?

I sat down to take a break and catch my breath and realized that I only had two gallons of water to last me the whole 18 hours so I would have to conserve. I needed a watch. It had only been about a half hour and I was beginning to get shaky. I hoped my mild hypoglycemia wasn't going to flare up. In high school the school nurse gave me a pass that would allow me to leave class at any time and go to the cafeteria and order a grilled cheese, milk and barbecue chips. I told her I had a mild dose of hypoglycemia. It helped. I would get very hungry. Like right now. What was I going to do without food for 18 hours? I decided I would wait it out and if I got desperate I would leave the tree and hunt for food. I was tired from all the jumping and from all the worrying, so I closed my eyes and leaned against the tree. If I didn't fall asleep at least I was conserving energy that I might need later in my search for food and shelter.

I tried to focus on my breathing and felt my hands and my fingers relax. It seemed as though I might be able to fall asleep so I tried to picture something pleasant. A few moments passed as I dreamed of buffets and affordable, delectable lunch specials at various Chinese restaurants in town. Then I began to look at the bald eagle feathers lying on the ground around me. I organized them into different patterns. I noticed my deerhide diaper and became cognizant of my moccasins and of the war paint on my face and body. In some strange way I was beginning to feel like a Native American. A lost Native American. I was Wounded Wolf and I was far from home. No one here really understood me. I closed my eyes and felt myself wandering around the forests of Oregon, far from my little apartment in Santa Barbara.

I began to dream deeply and think about the woman from San Nicolas Island, seventy miles off the coast of Santa Barbara. In 1835 she was one of a group of Indians who were being transferred off of the island. As the boat pulled away, she realized her baby had been

101

left behind. The boat's captain decided the surf was too dangerous to turn around and go back to the island. The woman, however, dived off the boat and began to swim back to the island. The last anyone saw of her was as she was swimming through the pounding surf towards the island. It was thought she had drowned in the rough seas, but eighteen years later, a group of seal hunters sailing off the coast of the island thought they spotted a woman on the shore. Word of the supposed sighting reached the mainland, and an expedition set out from Santa Barbara to check the island. They found her, alone. She had made it back to the island and found her child, but the child eventually died, as did all of the Indians who had been taken from the island.

I wondered about that woman and how her love of her child had overcome her fear and had thrust her overboard to swim back to shore. I wondered if her baby was alive when she made it back. How long did the baby live? What went through her mind for those eighteen years, alone on San Nicolas Island, her child and everyone she knew in the world gone. The searchers who found her brought her back to the mainland, but she died a few months later. During that time no one had successfully communicated with her, and she only spoke four words. I wonder what she did out there for eighteen years by herself. I'm by myself, but only for eighteen hours. I don't have a ship to jump from and swim to shore. I only have my tree. My enlightenment tree and I are being watched by two fake Shamans, not by seal hunters. So, maybe we are not all that much alike, but I was still thinking about her and feeling bad about what happened.

I could feel my hands beginning to shake like I'd had too much coffee, only that wasn't the case. I was just hungry and my blood sugar level was getting very low. I think I had been out in the forest in my diaper for at least three hours. I drank some water and begin to exercise again, this time doing push-ups and sit-ups and jumping jacks. I sat back down and looked at the eagle feathers and at my journal and decided to write some things down to kill the time:

Here I sit under my tree painted up like a warrior. I am shaking. I am hungry. I don't know what to do with myself. I don't want to think any more about this stupid trip and about my inner light and about who I want to become and about my issues and I am waiting for enlightenment. You know, I am thinking that maybe enlightenment takes more than a few hours, maybe even more than eighteen hours. Maybe it takes more than three days and maybe you can become enlightened without fasting and eating nuts and dressing up like a Native American. Maybe you don't have to wear deer-hide diapers. Maybe you can become enlightened while driving a cab in New York after eating a pepperoni pizza and having some coffee and a cigarette. Maybe a person could get into your cab and say something like, "You know, cabby, I'm really from the planet Zuno and it doesn't really matter where you take me because I am able to transmorph into thin air at any moment and get to the Plaza Hotel and order a Bombay Sapphire Martini."

That could be enough for a person to see the light and to think about mortality and pain and suffering and healing and ridding themselves of hunger and libido and desire for material things and envy. It certainly would be enough to make me think a little bit. You know, just driving around New York with a Zunite for a few minutes could do the trick. Or what if I was a truck driver or alone on a field driving a 1947 Cockshutt tractor made in Ontario, Canada. The thing doesn't move all that fast and I could be mesmerized by the hum of the engine and maybe drive into the night in that field and then right smack in the middle of a corn patch, flip on the lights and focus on the small bugs flying around, and find peace. You know the good kind of peace. But then again, what would I be doing in a field driving a Canadian tractor or in New York driving a cab? But, hey, what am I doing on the Rogue River in Oregon in deer-hide diapers covered in war paint? I don't know. But I'd like to.

I stopped writing because my hands were shaking and it was difficult for me to continue, so I laid down, foggy and fat. I was sweating and the dirt began to clump onto my skin and I could smell the pine tree all around me. It smelled like cherry pie a la mode. It figures the healer would set me up against a tree that smelled like a wonderful dessert. He probably knew the smell. In fact, they both are probably sitting back at camp wearing suits and ties working on laptops, cell phones up to their ears planning some other trip for honest people who are seeking to find some peace and to make some sense of things. The bastards. I began to hate them with the small amount of energy that I had left in me. Then, slowly, I fell asleep.

As my mind began to wander and paint pictures that even a kid could understand, I could feel my lips, dry and wind-chapped, begin to smile. I was laughing at myself and about how I was waiting to be enlightened. I was waiting for God or some inner-light or something to capture my body and change me forever. All I had to do was wait for eighteen hours. I started thinking about that number in my half-crazed, hypoglycemic daydreaming and I remembered that in Garland, Texas, there was a religious cult of 150 led by an ex-professor from Taiwan who had convinced his followers to move into a suburban district and buy up twelve homes. They would wait there until a certain day in March when God would appear on Channel 18 on any television set in the United States to announce his arrival on Earth the following week.

He would come to earth with a fleet of flying saucers and ferry everyone away from nuclear holocaust and flooding. I believe all the members were wearing white cowboy hats. God didn't show up for the interview. I felt like those people and I felt like the two Shamans were just like this ex-professor. Bright, possibly well-meaning people who had some power that made them able to control people. They had all bought homes outside of Dallas and followed this guy all the way from Taiwan. At least I only coughed up $1700 and took a short flight to Oregon.

I was beginning to feel sick. I started thinking about Father Diego in Ecuador and about the taxi driver who became a priest and about Peter's nephew and about the construction worker who lost his family and I felt like a complete idiot. They were real people seeking meaning, seeking God; I was just a dodo-bird running around with some tanned New Age cheerleader who happened to be in great physical shape. I decided I was going to get the hell out of Oregon and away from these freaks. I was tired and delirious five or six hours into my quest. I began to walk in the hope I would run into some campers or a family or those three guys on their vacation, borrow some clothes and see if they wouldn't help me get back to Santa Barbara. I had no choice. I now realized how stupid the whole thing was. This wasn't a spiritual quest, this was a way for two freaks to make a couple of thousand dollars and feed their spiritual ego until they got so fat they couldn't fit in a movie chair.

I began to wander and wander and progressively become weaker and weaker. I must have been walking for an hour when I smelled some type of smoke in the air. It smelled like burning wood or marijuana. As I walked the smell began to get stronger and stronger and it became clear to me that it was marijuana and then I began to hear laughter and talking. I was saved. I began to walk through a clearing in the forest where I saw a group of four young guys sitting around a campfire smoking what smelled like pot. As I walked toward the group I began to become conscious of my attire. My body and face were painted with mud and various colors of war paint. I was wearing moccasins and a small, ill-fitting diaper made of deer-hide and I was carrying three bald eagle feathers. To add to my concern I was walking into a campsite of what looked to be four college-age kids who by this point were stoned to the gills and laughing incessantly at how their tent looked like a Volkswagen Beetle only without the engine. I heard one say, "It doesn't even have an engine. Our tent doesn't have an engine. I can't believe this."

They were all bowled over laughing. What I didn't know was that they were four seniors from the Anthropology Department at the University of Oregon. I wish I would have known that before I walked up to their cannabis-filled world, dressed up like a Native American. I was just about to say hello, when one of them spotted me coming out from behind a tree. He put his hand up to tell the others to be quiet. Then all hell broke loose.

106

"Oh my God," one of them said, "it's Ishi!"

Ishi was the last remaining member of the Yahi tribe in northern California. In 1911, his tribe had been either killed off by white prospectors or had died of disease and/or starvation. When he realized that he was the only one left, he embarked on a suicide walk; he would begin to walk to the other end of the earth, and when he couldn't walk any more, he would lie down and die. One day a slaughterhouse employee found Ishi lying unconscious in the holding pen of the slaughterhouse. Ishi was eventually revived and brought back to health, but since he didn't speak English, or any known local Indian dialect (the Yahi tribe had their own language), the townspeople didn't know who he was, where he came from or where he belonged, so they lodged him in the town jail until they could figure out what to do with him. An anthropologist named Professor Waterman heard about Ishi and visited him in the jail there. Ishi took to the professor, and the first words he said were, "I ne ma Yahi," which means "I am a Yahi"—which, of course, meant nothing to people who had never heard of a Yahi.

Stoned out of his mind, one of these college students started chanting, "Ishi, Ishi, Ishi the Yahi."

All I could think of saying was, "I ne ma Yahi," which I probably shouldn't have said, but did anyway.

They were so stoned and filled with years of reading about Native Americans that they were 100% convinced they had discovered a lost tribesman, a new Ishi. If that's what they think, I thought, I might as well get something out of it. So I put two fingers up to my mouth, like I've seen people do in the movies, and rubbed my stomach. They began to run around the fire wildly, yelling at each other,

"He's hungry. Ishi is hungry, get him something to eat, get him something to eat!" This whole experience was a bit too much for one of the stoners, his mind overloaded by THC and the realization that he and his friends had stumbled upon a long-lost Indian warrior; he keeled over, unconscious.

"Let him sleep, let him sleep," the other one said. "He's not familiar with the Yahi Indians anyway."

So, I sat there, rubbing my stomach and squatting and putting my fingers up to my mouth and doing anything else I could think of to make them believe I was the new Ishi. They were so filled up with cannabis perfectus that my acting job was more than enough to convince them. Also, I was wearing a deer-hide diaper, moccasins and plenty of authentic war paint. They began to collect food, but to my dismay, they were doing so with a sense of cultural sensitivity.

"He can't process our food," one of them said, "So let's give him some nuts and berries from our trail mix bag and some water. I would love to give him a candy bar or a ham sandwich, but that would make him sick."

Great. My plan was fading before my eyes. I was so hungry, however, that if they fed me dirt with whipped cream on top I would have eaten it. They walked over to me, set some trail mix on the ground and quickly walked away. One of the cannabis worshippers said, "Let's not let our desire to discover Ishi get in the way of what we know about their culture and their inability to fight off the white man's disease. If we get too close to him or offer him a peace pipe, there is a good chance we could infect him and end up killing him. Let's not make the same mistakes our predecessors did. Ishi is a life, a soul, not a puppet or a toy. If we take him into captivity, into the hands of the undereducated, underpaid authorities, he will become nothing more than a circus sideshow exhibit, living the life of a historical prostitute, offering nothing but a cheap glance and an ooh-ahh to kids and adults who pay their five dollar entrance fee. No. That is not going to happen on my watch. We will smoke to him. Smoke for him. As the healing smoke rises and fades into the sky, let us watch him walk away, his beautiful back waving goodbye to modern ways. Ishi. Ishi our brother. We smoke for you. We smoke with you."

CHAPTER 8

They passed around a pipe, two or three times and when the stuff hit them, they all sat down Indian style and motioned for me to go back to where I came from. Then, one by one, they laid down around the fire and fell into a deep, self-satisfied, marijuana-induced sleep.

There I was, sitting with four completely stoned anthropology students who had gone the way of the peaceful warrior and I was hungry, frustrated and tired. I began to walk around the campsite looking for food. I found a roast beef sandwich and some chips, which I devoured in about two seconds, then found some homemade beer. What is it with these people in the Pacific Northwest? Can't they drink a Budweiser once in a while? They are so smitten with the microbrew syndrome they can't see straight.

I had to make some choices. I could wander back to my enlightenment tree, if I could even find it, or I could wait here for them to wake up from their slumber, explain the whole situation to them and ask them to take me to the nearest train station. Or I could borrow their lovely VW bus with drapes and bumper stickers that read "Powered by Cannabis" and "Friends don't let friends shop at Barnes and Noble." I sat there for a few minutes and tried to brainstorm a solution to this problem. I made my choice. Considering my situation—almost hallucinating from hypoglycemia (or maybe a contact high from the weed my audience had been smoking)—it was pretty much the only choice I could make: I grabbed my three bald eagle feathers and two jars of their homemade beer and stole the VW bus. Before I continue, it is important to note that under regular circumstances I would not have stolen a car, especially not a VW bus. But when you think about making good choices in life, ethical, moral choices, you never find yourself having to make them half-stoned, hungry and dressed up like Ishi. So I drove off on a dirt road, hoping the four students would stay asleep long enough for me to get into town, stash the VW and hop a bus, plane or train back to Santa Barbara.

My plan failed miserably. I found my way out to a main road and had been driving about twenty minutes when I noticed a police car in back of me. I was hoping he was just one of those cops who tails hippies for the fun of it, but soon the siren blared and his roof lights flared on and off; he wanted me to pull over. It was time for me to make another major decision. I had to take stock. Here I was, dressed like a long-lost Indian, full of the effects of home-made beer and a contact high, driving a vehicle that was not mine that had bumper stickers proclaiming, "Powered by cannabis." Things were not looking very good. I pulled over.

"License and reg … whoa, there! You on your way to the fair or something?"

"Yes, sir, I am."

"You in one of them Indian shows?"

"Yes, sir, you should come down and check it out."

"Ah hell, I'd love to, but ever since my eye surgery I haven't been able to take all the lights and such at the carnivals. It's a shame, too, cause I love the cotton candy and the haunted house and all."

My stomach began to pant and heave.

"What type of surgery did you have?" I asked.

"Well, some quack and his Commie sidekick convinced me to get some laser surgery up in Washington to correct my nearsightedness. Now because of them, every darn night at the same time I start seeing a whole herd of dancing pink elephants. Can you believe it?"

"Oh gosh," I said, "that's terrible."

"You got your license and reg in your diaper there, bud?"

"No, sir, I don't. This here is our leader's car and I'm just back from town bringing the group some more drums and feathers. My wallet is at the fair in my clothes. I'm sorry."

"Sorry?" he said. "Did you know that I could ticket you and haul you downtown for not having a license and reg on you?"

"No, sir, I did not know that, but now I do and I won't let it happen again."

He started walking around the car, looking at the plates and the bumper stickers and all, and said, "My nephew works at Barnes & Noble. Why doesn't your leader want his friends to shop there?"

"Good question, sir. He is a little weird. I shop there all the time, in fact I was just there yesterday."

"Which store?" he asked.

"The one there in town."

"Cedar Creek or Mill Valley?" he asked.

"Mill Valley," I said, hoping that was the right answer.

"That's where Eric works," he said. "I'll be. I'll tell you what. You seem like a nice enough guy, all dressed up and all. I'm gonna let you off this time because I know how important the fair is to the children and they'd be missin' out if you was sittin' at the station. El comprendamendo?"

"Yes, comprendamendo."

Then he waddled his double-cheeseburger-and Budweiser-filled belly back to his car and radioed in that he was heading home. His shift was over and he needed to get back to Bessie before the elephants began to dance.

So, shaking, I drove on to the sounds of bootlegged Grateful Dead. I was actually feeling pretty good, considering my situation. I drove into what looked like a small town, parked outside a diner and searched the bus to find out what I could borrow in terms of clothes and money. I intended to somehow give it all back. I found a T-shirt that said, "Got Pot?" and I borrowed some gray sweats and found some sandals. I rubbed the war paint off my face and arms with a towel and stepped out of the van into civilization. It was nice to be away from the healers and back where my name was Simeon and not Wounded Wolf and where I was allowed to talk.

I had a major cash flow problem, however. I could only find two dollars in change. So I walked away from the car and started looking around. There was a bunch of booths on the far end of the town in a small park and behind them was the Orcutt Fair. You could feel the buzz of excitement that had turned this little town into a block of smiles and shaved ice and churros and taffy. I walked over to the booths, thinking the whole time that I had to come up with some sort of plan. I mean, I had just stolen a car, I was broke and I was trying to escape a vision quest complete with Shamans and fasting. Out of the corner of my eye I saw a crowd of Native Americans, real Native Americans, outside a booth labeled, "The Native Council on New Age Shamans"—TNCNAS, for short. That was interesting, especially considering my current plight. I walked up to the booth and an older man with deep, dark eyes and weathered skin looked up at me with bad teeth and handed me a flyer as he said, "We are spreading the word, Ya, to keep New Age Shamans out of our ancestral holy sites and from using our sacred names. Take this information, Ya, and tell people. It is a disgrace to our people and our heritage." He looked down at his grandson holding on to his chair and smiled at him.

I walked away with the pamphlet and wondered what he would have thought if he could have seen me half an hour earlier with my war paint and diapers. I sat there for a minute, a few feet back from the booth. I read the information and began to realize what I was taking part in on the vision quest weekend. I didn't have the strength to grasp all the ramifications of what I was reading but I was taken by one sentence: "We cannot continue to charge tourists to watch and gawk at our sacred Sun Dances and take money from people who want to exploit our traditions to fill a void in their own lives. This is our tradition, our religion, our history. It is not something that can be purchased."

I walked away, dejected and tired. I turned toward the stolen van because I couldn't take any more reality and slowly made my way back to the parking lot in front of the diner. I sat there, with my Got Pot? T-shirt, sitting up high in the seat of the bus with my hands on the steering wheel, and made the first mature decision I had made in a long time. I was going to take the car back to the stoned anthropology students, face the music and find my way back to the Enlightenment Tree, where I would wait to be picked up by the fake Shamans and then somehow get back home with the group. It was decided.

I found the dirt road that had taken me to the main highway and put the car in first gear and slowly drove back to the campsite. I think God was watching over me, because they were still asleep when I pulled up, and I slowly took off their clothes, put the money back into the ashtray, dressed up in my diaper and moccasins and walked back into the forest. I wondered if they would even remember Ishi and the whole experience. I wondered what they would be thinking when they woke from their THC-induced slumber. I didn't really care, though, I just wanted to find the tree and sit there until I would be picked up. I turned back to look at the campsite and started to think about the students and about the old man at the Native American booth and I looked down at my moccasins and began to laugh and then, slowly, I could feel tears welling up in my eyes.

I continued to walk, aimlessly. I was beginning to understand what was going on. I just didn't care anymore. I didn't care about the stupid gym, about Elena, about the two fake Shamans, about my dumb college pal, Wandering Duck, or whatever his name was, and about anything that had been going on. I didn't care if they found me walking toward the tree or eating a Philly cheese steak. I didn't want to talk to them anymore and I certainly didn't want them to exploit my emotions any longer. They didn't really care, anyway. Why should I let them into my life and why did I put myself into this bizarre situation? Then, because I think someone was watching over me, I found the tree and sat there and closed my eyes, took a deep breath and put my hands together in a defeated pose. It was not the pose of a lion.

I must have fallen asleep because the next thing I remember was a tap on my shoulder and two fake Shamans standing over me grabbing my hands and pulling me up. I didn't even react because I couldn't muster up the energy to care as we walked back the mile or so to camp. The camp was already cleaned up, the boat was loaded up and Alan was sitting in the boat, looking like he had just been beaten up. Evidently he had gone a little haywire out there and had run through some bushes and scratched and cut himself. I guess that is why they came and got me a little early. The rest of the day was like a dream. I got into the boat and listened to the water splash against the front and looked over at wounded Alan and at the two freaks and then I looked away. I didn't want to talk or feel, or think or wonder. We got back to the base camp at the head of the Rogue River and there was a picnic table with juice and chicken and nuts and cookies and water and we all sat down and began to eat like barbarians. Poor Alan was having a hard time. We were both shaking. Then B.D. spoke.

"You have both been through something incredible. You will not be able to understand what happened for a few days. What I want you to think about is how lucky you are to have explored yourself so deeply, without the effects of chemicals or food or shelter. Most people go their entire lives in front of the television, eating frozen meals and listening to the hum of their children playing and don't get the chance to connect with their inner-force. We are going to get in the van and head home, and then, later in the week, we are going to get together and talk about your re-entry into society and about what went on here. You don't have to talk on the way home. Just sit and be with your light."

The truth is I didn't have enough energy to even respond to his stupidity. I was so tired of his voice and I couldn't believe his sham of a partner anymore. They were both the worst kind of people, so self-absorbed that they really thought they were doing the right thing, taking our money, giving us a hodgepodge of different religious and psychological strains and molding them all together into a meaningless yet destructive glob. I wanted to fight both of them, and Alan along with them, because in some way I felt like he was a part of the whole thing, part of the scam to get me involved in this stupid Pure USA Gym. When anyone looked at me, I stared them down and made painstaking eye contact, like they tell you to do in an interview. The sick part about this journey home was that in the minds of B.D. and his car salesman cohort, I was acting distant and aggressive because I had come so far on my spirit journey. I was a changed man and having trouble re-acclimating. It probably made them feel good that I was so aggravated. They felt successful. How do people become so delusional, so out of touch with reality, so saturated with their own growth and success that they drown in it and pull everyone around them down with them? I was getting out of this mysterious gym and group forever. I was going back to writing about tractors and my Greek and talking to Peter and hanging out with his rocket-launching nephew and that was it. No more Elena and her sweet-smelling brown skin. No more trying to win her over by going on trips with her psychotic lover and no more meetings. If I learned anything from the fasting and the dressing up like a Native American it was that when you are hungry, you should eat, and unless you are invited to a costume party, regular clothes will do just fine.

We walked to the van to take the short trip to the airport, where we boarded a plane to San Francisco and from there headed home to Santa Barbara. I had begun to cool down by the time I got off the plane at the Santa Barbara airport, until we walked into the parking lot and I got a glimpse of the woman who started the greatest war in the history of western civilization. She was tan, again, brown and smiling and thinking about loving me until the cows came home. She ran up to B.D. and hugged him and kissed him and when they were pulling apart I noticed her hands playfully pinching his concave and minuscule butt. I cracked my neck in a show of protest. I looked at the ground and rolled my shoulders and pulled on my shirt as if I didn't care. I wanted to smash everyone in the group. I took a deep breath and said, "Hi, Elena."

"Hi, Sym," she said with a smile. "Did you guys have fun?"

"Loads," I said, shaking my head, and then B.D. whispered something in her ear, probably about my aggression and how far I had come and how much of my light and inner-force I was now aware of. Little did he know I ate roast beef sandwiches, drank home-made beer, stole a car from four stoned anthropology students, got pulled over and ended up at a Native American booth bent on prosecuting sacrilegious trespassers like him. I smiled at that. I got in the car and prayed I would get home without Elena and B.D. groping each other in the front seat of the van. They dropped me off at the gym and as I nudged my way around Alan to the door, Elena said,

"I hope your car starts, Sim."

"I do, too," I said, and then, for some unknown reason, I blurted out, "I hope you go home with him tonight and think about me."

I couldn't believe I said it. I was so proud of myself. B.D. looked at me, and I was hoping he would get out of the car and try something, but he just smiled like guys like him do and said, "You've had a tough weekend, Sim, get some rest and we will talk with you on Wednesday."

He put his arm around the harlot and they drove away.

CHAPTER 9

Monday was a gray day. I had stayed up until 2:00 a.m. drinking Meister Brau and smoking menthol cigarettes. I had reached an all-time low. I had done so well not smoking for almost three months, but the whole weekend threw me off balance. I woke up around 9:00 with a sick feeling that I had called Peter and talked to him about everything. When I noticed how many beer cans were strewn about my apartment, I began to realize I didn't remember anything we had talked about. Great.

I made my way, slowly and with my head pounding, to the coffee shop by the office. I shook as I grabbed the crumpled dollar bills in my jeans and looked at the counter to avoid all contact with human beings. I stumbled up to the office and hoped to God that Andrew, Peter's nephew, wasn't going to be in the office on this day. I opened the door.

"Hey, sunshine," said Peter. "How are you feeling?"

"Not so hot," I said as I sat down at my desk.

"Kind of a cloudy day for sunglasses, isn't it?" he asked with a smile.

"Yeah, I guess," I replied with guilt.

"I told Andrew to enjoy the town today because I didn't think you would be in any condition to meet him."

"Thanks, Peter," I said. "I was worried about that."

He put his hand on my shoulder and placed an editorial run-sheet on my desk and left me alone. I felt an overwhelming sense of gratitude. I probably kept him up 'til all hours of the night, babbling on about who knows what, but he didn't seem to hold that against me and, in fact, seemed to sympathize with me. I had the feeling he was pretty sure that I hadn't spent the weekend visiting my mother. I decided to break the ice.

"You know, Peter, I wasn't in North Dakota this weekend."

"I know," he said, "you told me all about it last night."

"Did I tell you what I said to Elena?"

"About five times," he said and walked into his office.

"I'm sorry I called you in that condition."

"Don't worry about it, I'm glad you did."

And that was it. That was all the interrogation I got for the day. I probably told him about the entire weekend and about all kinds of things, so he was full of enough information for a while. I stared at the computer for a few hours, answered the phone and questions about what would be the best tractor to convert into a combine race machine, and then tried to start on my first story for the month.

Peter must have known I needed a break, or at least some comic relief, when he assigned me the story about Dr. Diesel. This is a singer who had a small measure of success in the country-and-western circuit around Tulsa and was taking on the hip-hop movement from the bucket seat of a tractor. He is the farmer's version of Vanilla Ice. He is thirty-two years old, divorced and writing rap lyrics about farming and tractors and crops and soil and pesticides. I think he's loco, but he just got signed by Capitol Records and is touring farm festivals and being interviewed by every AM radio station from Nevada to Maine. He's a cult hero. I heard about him when I went to that Diesel Cacti Gathering in Mesa, but I thought he was a novelty. No, he was the real thing. After a few phone conversations and listening to his first album once or twice I came up with this story:

Who says farmers can't rap? Who says we can't dance? Who says we can't take on the hip-hop movement from our fields a-plenty? Who says a man can't dance and feel and prod that funky beat to be heard around the nation? This is a tractor magazine, but we got to tell you, we found a man, a tractor-owning man at that, who is taking the music world by storm. He's young, he's dirty and he's a farmer. Meet Dr. Diesel.

Born in Tulsa in 1968 to a corn farmer and a schoolteacher, Rando Jansen—a.k.a. Dr. Diesel—began his music career playing the flute in the Jackson County High School band. He then went on to a job at Radio Shack where he became acquainted with the karaoke machine. On his breaks and when the customer rush was low, Dr. Diesel would slap in Helen Reddy's "I Am Woman" or the Rolling Stones' "Satisfaction" and belt away. This went on for months, until the good Doc decided he had stumbled upon his future. He started singing with country bands, and a short time later, he had a vision. He described it to me: "I was sitting in the dirt, tired, bewildered, my throat dry from the singing of city folks' songs and it hit me. I need to write from the dirt, from the tractor, from the field. And I'm gonna do it in that hip-hop format." That was 1997. Three years later he is the talk of the farming community. People who thought dancing was for wackos are shaking their groove thing. Old men, old women, kids and teens are rockin' to his funky beat. His most popular song, "Get That Thing and Drive It," about the fear of driving a tractor, is being played all over the airwaves.

> *Woop. woop. That thing. Get it.*
> *You got boots. You got jeans.*
> *Woop. That thing. Get it.*
> *You got time. The corn ain't leavin*
> *Get that thing and drive it.*

He's huge and ready to rock the hip-hop world with his combination of good moves, good lyrics and the heart of a farmer. He might not be the new Michael Jackson, but when was the last time the gloveless wonder made it out to Tulsa?

Peter liked the story. In fact, he loved the whole idea of Dr. Diesel, so he got together with the advertising department and set up a subscription plan that included a free CD from Dr. Diesel with every renewal. That meant the good doctor would have to visit our office for a photo shoot and to discuss the matter further. I was looking forward to meeting him. And, I would find out later, so was Peter. There was more to the subscription promotion than I knew about.

I made it home that evening, wolfed down some Top Ramen and hit the sack. I was still hung over and depressed from the weekend. I turned off the ringer. When I got up for work the next day there was a message from B.D. inviting me over to his house on Wednesday to talk about the weekend. I didn't want to go. I hated him. I hated his stupid Porsche-selling partner and I hated myself for believing in those guys and the entire gym. It was becoming clear to me that they were just a 24-hour real-life infomercial, convincing tired people that their product would bring them the joy and peace they had been searching for. Then I thought back and realized I had joined the gym in the middle of the night because of an infomercial, and the whole thing began to make sense. They sucked me into the whole scheme. It was my fault for being up at four in the morning eating a large pepperoni pizza. But I was hungry. I got dressed and made it to the office. Today was the day I got to meet Peter's rocket-launching nephew, Andrew-the-letter-writer.

I walked into the office and Peter and Andrew were sitting at my desk, working on my computer. Andrew didn't look anything like I expected. He was tall and thin. I don't know why but I pictured him as short and a little stocky. He was wearing a blue V-neck sweater with a white T-shirt underneath, baggy tan pants, gray socks and Birkenstock sandals. His eyes were brown and piercing. I was instantly amazed by him and what he did with those rockets.

"Hey, Sim," said Peter. "this is Andrew."

"It's nice to meet you, Andrew," I said. "I've heard a lot about you from Peter."

"It's nice to meet you, Simeon. I hope you don't mind us sitting at your desk," he said.

"Not at all," I demurred as I walked to Peter's office and put my stuff down. I couldn't believe how confident and calm and mature he was. I couldn't picture him in a nuthouse, he seemed too normal.

The day went on and I spent most of it editing my story on Dr. Diesel and working on an inspirational story about the drought that was now taking place in North Dakota and comparing it to the one that took place in the 1930s. It was an interesting story for me to work on because my family originated in North Dakota and my mom was working in Richardton. My grandma was born in Richardton, where her father was a farmer and a shop owner. I thought about making it a personal article, with a personal story, but I'm not sure I wanted to reveal anything to the majority of the tractor reading public. They might take it the wrong way, think I'm a sissy and not able to effectively test and rate earth-moving machines like a man should. I don't know.

I called my mom to talk about that year when the rains didn't come and about the effect the current drought was having, and we got to talking about my grandma as a little girl and about how hard it was for my mom to watch her fade away in a retirement home, dying of colon cancer. "She is very old," I kept telling her, but I guess age doesn't matter when you're watching your mom die. I don't want to die; in fact, I think about it a lot when I drive or fly and wonder if old people like my grandma know it's coming. I wonder if they're scared. I know my mom is filled with fear as she holds on to her shaking hands while my grandma stares at her like a ghost. She is always shaking. I decided to maybe add a family anecdote into the story but I would figure it out later.

After the call, we began to talk about lunch, as we usually do, and decided to go to the Chinese Kingdom. I love the Chinese Kingdom and was sure Andrew would like it as well. While we were walking I started to think about the last time I was there with Elena, that day when she got up and left me sitting at the table. The same table that held the small tea cup that insisted on showing me my dad's aging face and all of that. Maybe Chinese wasn't such a good idea. What about Mexican? I didn't want to display too many of my issues to the young Andrew at our first luncheon, so I bit my lip and sauntered into the restaurant with my two friends. Disaster struck. Elena and some older guy were sitting in the corner of the restaurant. He was heavy, had a black beard, a ponytail and was wearing a black shirt, black pants and a leather vest. I almost vomited. "Peter," I whispered, shaking, "that is Elena."

I didn't know what to do, but I knew I needed to do something. I walked over to her and tried to be as calm and confident as I possibly could and, thankfully, Peter didn't follow, realizing the severity of the situation. She waved.

"Hi, Sim, what are you guys doing here?"

"We just came down to get some lunch." I couldn't think of anything else to say so I just stood there and the fat old guy continued to eat as if I didn't even exist, so like a scorned man I put my hand out.

"How ya doing, I'm Simeon." He put his fork down and grabbed my hand with a death grip.

"I'm Jojo." He looked at me for a second and then continued eating.

"You guys have a good lunch," I said with as much courage as I could muster and walked back to the table, completely confused and nauseous. I mean, this was pretty much all my fault. I don't even know this girl yet I allowed myself to fall in love with her. I don't know who she really is. I was just awestruck by her eyes and her body and her voice and the way she smells and that she's from deep, dark South America and I had been there and on and on. Who was this guy? Was she sleeping with him? Was she sleeping with B.D.? Of course she was. She was sleeping with half the town and all the while I thought she was in love with me. She sleeps with people for a living. She's a sleeper. I hate her and all her sex and all the men she sexes. How does she get the energy? Probably all that working out at the stupid Pure USA Gym. I wanted to tell B.D. he had a sleeper in his employ and I found the whole thing out. She couldn't even have lunch with me but yet she could sleep with the entire town without much effort. All the while she was holding down a full-time job at the gym. I was beginning to get dizzy. She must know everything there is to know about sleeping with men. She's a sex genius. I sat down with my two friends.

"Hallo, welcome to the Kingdom. Something to drink today?"

"No," I said with half the world on my shoulders.

"He will have a Tsing Tao and we would like two Cokes," Peter said.

"Do you normally drink at lunch?" Andrew asked innocently.

"No," I said and took a deep, yoga-inspired breath, "only when I discover the girl I love is a hooker."

"Oh," he said. Peter smiled at me and grabbed his chopsticks.

"Guess what?" he said, trying desperately to change the subject. "We're going on a field trip tomorrow."

I loved field trips.

"Where are we going?" Andrew asked.

"Well, Dr. Diesel is coming over tonight and we're going to make the single greatest Spam recipe known to man and all of us are driving down to the Los Angeles County Fair tomorrow and entering it into the Spam Recipe Contest."

I felt sick.

"They have a contest for Spam recipes?" I asked.

"Oh yeah, it's huge. Last year I guess they had over 500 entries."

"Wow," said Andrew.

I just looked down and tried to decide between Two Flavor Szechuan, Kung Pao Beef or Imperial Shrimp. The problem with ordering shrimp for the lunch special is quantity. You could end up with only five shrimp on your plate hidden in a mountain of unnamed vegetables and lettuce-like objects. I wasn't willing to take that chance. Not today. I decided to go with the beef because it was the most manly thing I could do and, considering I was in love with a hooker and drinking at lunch, it made sense to complete the scenario.

"Is that your girlfriend over there with the heavy-set guy?" Andrew asked.

"She's not really my girlfriend, I just fell in love with her for various reasons and now am paying for it."

"Paying for what?" he asked.

"For the fact that she is a hooker of sorts," I said.

"I dated a hooker once," he said as Peter began to choke on his hot tea.

"She was in the rocket launching club I was involved with. She was so beautiful and sweet and small and innocent-looking. I loved her. In fact, I wrote some letters to her, which I'm sure you have heard about.

"I heard something about that, but..."

"Well, she used to move from RV to RV a lot when we were out at the desert launching rockets, but she told me she had a lot of relatives in the group so I didn't think anything of it. Ends up she was sharing her sacred gift with a few of the other launchers for money. She loved me, though, or so she said. It's terrible to think about now, all those men and all those RVs and rockets launching all over the place. No wonder I needed some time to get my head together. I'm supposed to talk about my past, according to my therapist, so I thought I'd share that."

I began to feel really bad for Andrew. I might have exaggerated a bit with Elena. I don't really know if she is a hooker, in fact I can't imagine she is, and it prompted Andrew to spill the beans. Now I felt worse than ever. Andrew didn't look so good. Then Elena and JoJo walked over and she introduced herself to Peter and Andrew while JoJo cleaned his gums with a toothpick.

"You must be Peter," she said. "And you must be Andrew." I had told her about them both.

"Nice to meet you," they said simultaneously.

129

"I don't date hookers," Andrew said and I went for my beer and took an enormous swig.

"Excuse me?" she said.

"I'm not interested in dating any more hookers," Andrew said. I began to sweat and pant. But, in her supernatural kindness, she put her hand on his shoulder and said,

"Someone as cute and kind as you will find a beautiful girl someday who will love you." Andrew began to blush and then he twitched and looked angry and said, "I appreciate that, but my point is, I'm not going to pay for it." I almost died in my chair.

"You won't ever have to," she said with a kind smile. They walked away. I was stunned. I had heard from Peter that one of the things Andrew was supposed to work on was his timing of certain comments. He had the newfound habit of telling it as he saw it, without much deference to tact. I didn't know what to do. Peter sat back in his chair and pretended to read the menu but I knew what he was thinking about. I should have been upset about the JoJo encounter but instead I was stunned by Andrew's dry humor or anger or whatever it was. We ordered and it became painfully silent. "She doesn't look like a hooker," Andrew said.

"You know, Andrew, I'm not so sure she really is a hooker. I think I might have exaggerated a little bit and I'm sorry if I caused you to think that was the case."

"That's okay, Simeon, I know what you meant." And that was all that was said on that topic. We spoke a little bit more about the Spam contest and the field trip and then we went back to work for the day. I honestly didn't know what to think. I was secretly happy that Andrew had said those things even though they were extremely odd and ill timed; I would have never had the courage to even consider saying them. Maybe she did have more than one overnight guest, I don't know. Maybe she was a prostitute, with her emotions if not with her body. I don't know. I went home and changed into my Spam T-shirt that Peter had given me compliments of the Hormel Corporation, and made my way to the Spam party with Peter, Dr. Diesel and Andrew.

CHAPTER 10

I knocked on the door of Peter's house and heard someone walk up to get the door and then I heard singing. "Who can it be knocking at my door?" he sang. "Go away, don't come round here no more. Can't you see that it's late at night? I'm very tired. And I'm not feelin right." And then he laughed and opened the door with flair. "I'm better at rapping. I'm Rando, you must be Simeon."

"Hi, Rando. You look nothing like I pictured."

"I trust that is a good thing," he said.

"A very good thing," I answered. And we walked into the kitchen.

I said hello to Peter who was wearing a dangerously-colored Spam apron and explaining the recipe to Andrew, who was listening attentively. For a moment I was concerned for Andrew and the stability of Peter's home but I put that thought behind me. It was clear to me Peter loved Andrew as an uncle should, even though he was wearing a mauve apron and falling in love with Rando the rapper.

Andrew had to see how much Peter cared for him and how healthily he invited him into his home and work and how kindly he was treating him. I noticed it and it made me value Peter's friendship even more. He continued to discuss the recipe with us all in order to drum up enthusiasm for the contest that would take place in Los Angeles the following morning. He began to preach to us as we sat on the countertop:

"People approach these contests in two ways. The first group goes overboard, pretending that Spam really is a world-renowned delicacy and create French and Spanish dishes hiding Spam's salty quality. We are not going to do that." He was using a lot of hand motions.

"The second group see Spam as a condiment or something worthy of ridicule so they marginalize the Spam, and, in doing so, create boring and uneventful recipes, like Spam sandwiches and Spam quesadillas or Spamburgers. We are not going to do that either. We know who we are and what Spam is and we are going to make what Rando and I have decided to call Spamdorf Salad. It is the original Waldorf complete with nuts and lots of mayonnaise, but with large and well-manicured pieces of Spam Lite included. In our recipe, Spam is not overdone and it is not marginalized. It is utilized for what it is, a very popular brand of spiced ham."

Rando clapped enthusiastically and Peter bowed to each of us. I was impressed by the speech and with the thought that went into the decision to create the Spamdorf Salad. I hoped the final product would convey Peter's rationale. The judges at these contests are brutal, or so I've heard. We all went into the kitchen and Rando began to rap, free-form, while dancing around the kitchen,

> You don't call me Waldorf
> You don't call me Spam
> All you need to know farm daddy
> is that together Spam I am

This Rando guy had a real flair for entertaining. No wonder he had become such a huge hit. Andrew left and was in the living room watching television, so I left the kitchen, the home of the fanatic-Spamatics, and sat down next to him. He was watching a public access show. In front of the poorly put together set and in between the bad lighting was a blonde woman holding a snake and talking about spirit journeys. I felt sick.

"Can you change it, Andrew? I just spent an entire weekend that looked and felt like that lady with the snake. I'd rather forget about it if it's okay with you."

"No problem," Andrew said. "Peter told me all about your weekend. It sounded very weird."

"It was," I said.

The next morning I heard the honk of the pink Thunderbird. It was a tight fit but the four of us made it into the car and the Spamdorf Salad was tightly positioned in the trunk. Peter had created a refrigerator out of blue ice and foil. The salad needed to keep for almost three hours until the competition. He also brought another set of ingredients, which he hadn't tossed, in case the first salad looked worn. Presentation is vital at all Spam events.

As we walked into the halls of the famous L.A. County Fair I could taste the salty ham in my nostrils. Spam was everywhere and most everyone was smiling. The L.A. County Fair is a huge production but from an outsider's point of view, the Spam Recipe Contest had to be one of the largest draws. People were busily preparing their recipes, talking about and tasting Spam and nervous about the results. Andrew and I walked around while Peter and Rando put the finishing touches on the Spamdorf. Spam recipe contests are very well organized. You set up your dish at a specified table and then you wait for the judges to go around and choose the semifinalists. They judge on presentation, creativity and taste.

Rando was especially excited because he ran into a woman at the contest who had known his mother when she was younger. Evidently, Jay Hormel organized a group of sixty ex-service women into a dance troupe that toured county fairs and other events around the nation spreading the news about the new spiced ham product. Rando's mom was an alternate in the group. She was only called in a few times when one of the regulars was ill, but she could call herself a Hormel Girl and be telling the truth. I realized then that we were here because of Rando and his mother, not because Peter had gone the way of the loons.

We waited with great anticipation for the judges to make their decision. Fifteen dishes were chosen out of the hundreds of entries. And, because I think Rando had some pull with Hormel, the

Spamdorf made it into the semifinal round. We walked up to the semifinalist area and Peter gracefully put down the dish next to a card that read "Dish #7." Fifteen anxious people and their friends and family stood around as the Spam experts tasted and talked and took notes. Rando looked nervous. Peter was fidgeting. Andrew looked like he was on the moon driving one of those four-wheel-drive golf carts with huge tires.

Then the three judges made their way up to, and took bites from, the Spamdorf. We all held our breaths. They chewed slowly, stoic and determined, made a few notes and proceeded. I tried to watch their facial expressions to get a clue. Not these judges. They could have thought the Spamdorf was the single greatest thing since Spam Lite was introduced. And it turned out they did. The glorious Spamdorf, created by Peter and Rando, *Man Tractors* editor and amateur chef and the rapping son of a former alternate Hormel Girl, took first prize in the Spam Recipe contest at the L.A. County Fair. They were elated. Peter told the Hormel representatives enthusiastically, "I've never won anything in my life." We were all very happy. Peter and Rando collected the prize money, signed some papers and found out that they would be flown to Dallas, Texas, in a month to compete in the National Championship. I couldn't believe it. I wasn't quite sure what I was doing at the fair in the first place and to be part of the winning team in a Spam recipe contest made me feel even stranger.

I started looking around at all the people who had made the drive from different parts of California with their Spam recipes stuffed gracefully somewhere in the car. It was a Spam caravan. Up and down the California coast, Spam warriors prepared for the ultimate battle. Weeks and weeks of battle training was to end in minutes of elation or sorrow at the hands of the three war judges. Who was most prepared? Who had entered the battle with the proper ingredients, the creative flare needed to win the battle and who, most importantly would win the taste game? In the end, my boss and his rapping special friend came out victorious. And, I, as well as young Andrew the former basket case, was part of the winning team. We were military intelligence, behind the scenes, not on the front lines, but vital, integral to the eventual victory. As we were ferried away in the pink battleship, back up the coast to Santa Barbara, our flags were flying proudly, our horn was honking and Rando the rapper was letting loose with Spam-inspired free verse. I was a winner, I was a warrior, I was Simeon, Simeon the Spam sympathizer circling the walled city after glorious victory, dragging my war booty for all to see.

When I got home my elation and battle euphoria had turned into nothing more than a smile at how my day had been spent. I had been putting off calling B.D. back about getting together. In fact, I'm sure I missed the meeting during the week. It had taken me a while to get over that weekend; I don't know if I will ever completely get over it. I was still thinking about Elena a little bit and how she ran up to the tanned one at the airport and hugged him and playfully touched him. I think maybe I was a tiny little diversion for her. Maybe she was mad at B.D. or maybe he had hurt her and she used me to remind herself that she was desirable, and then, knowing that, she felt complete enough to go back to the freak. In some strange way I had led her back to the snake. In some way, I was responsible, because I let it happen, I let her use my passion for her as fuel, as diversionary fuel that pushed her slowly but inevitably back to the fake Menehune healer, gym owner, therapist, drum maker and complete jerk. To make matters worse, after the airport fondling, in a state of complete delusion, I sent her a card with a crushed red rose and a poem by Rilke. This is what I said:

Dear Elena. I saw tonight that you are in love with B.D. and that whatever happened between us is no longer. I wish it were different, but something inside, even if it is a whisper, tells me it is for the better. I read this poem the other night and it made me think of the night we spent together at the winery.

> *You don't know nights of love. Don't*
> *petals of soft words float upon your blood?*
> *Are there no places on your dear body*
> *that keep remembering like eyes.*
> *(Ranier Maria Rilke, Paris, summer 1909)*

I had no idea she would show the card and the poem to B.D.

But that is exactly what she did. I had called B.D. on Monday to tell him I didn't need to come to a meeting and to say thanks but no thanks and I think I wanted to break up with him and the gym. Why I didn't just disappear into a sweet hiatus of tractors and Ancient Greek courses is beyond me, but I felt like the polite thing to do was to call. Big mistake. In his regular manipulative fashion he complimented me and told me how well I did on the trip and many other things that, in the end, added up to me committing to a meeting with him and Alan and the other Shaman, Fred, on Tuesday night. Little did I know that I was walking into a trap. I saw the meeting as closure for me. I thought I would go, listen to the wrap-up of the weekend and tell them all, including my college buddy Alan, that it was over, that I didn't want to be a part of the group anymore and that I had decided it would be much cheaper if I just went on a walk once or twice a week. I also had planned on telling them that my Greek courses were becoming more challenging, which they were, and that I needed to focus more on school and less on my body and spirit. There were plans in place, but none of them could have prepared me for the battle dome that I walked into on Tuesday night.

I put on a very comfortable outfit that included jeans, a white undershirt and a tan baggy sweater. I rubbed white musk oil on my wrists and neck and made sure that I left the house with wet hair. I was fresh, and soon, I would be free. I found B.D.'s house up in the Mesa area of Santa Barbara. I wasn't that impressed with the decorations, mostly pictures of himself and paintings he had done. Typical. We all sat down in a small living room that was filled with incense smoke and various, pre-paid long distance degrees framed on the wall. I was the first to arrive, but Alan knocked on the door soon after I sat down. Fred was in the kitchen getting some tea together and B.D. was wandering around the house in a confident but agitated manner.

Then the Ecuadorian traitor walked into the room and back into my life. She looked so beautiful and I could smell her from twenty feet away. Her hair was wet and she was pulling up the sleeves of her yellow sweater because she had just put it on. I smiled at her and forgot about everything but how beautiful she was and how I wanted to touch her and make her mine. But she walked right by me with a stunned look on her face and didn't even wave or anything. I put my head down in defeat. This was going to be an interesting evening. Once again I was in enemy territory, not on my own turf, subject to various subtle forms of abuse and belittlement. But I chose to be there, I was there for the big break-up, to tell the guru and his harlot mama that it is over, and to say goodbye to Alan the vodka thief and to wish Vic good luck with Kara and his life. We all sat down together and B.D. told us Vic couldn't join us and that he and Kara had moved out of the country to go live with her aunt in Sweden. I don't blame them. So, there we were in B.D.'s living room, Alan, Fred, B.D. and Elena and I. I stood up and decided I was going to make the whole thing short and sweet,

"Before we get started I just want to say that I've learned a lot from this group, but I don't want to be a part of all of this anymore. I want to shake all your hands tonight and give Elena a hug and get back to my schooling and work as soon as possible."

B.D. said, "That's nice, Simeon, but judging from this letter here that you sent to my woman, it seems clear you want to do more than just hug Elena goodbye." I didn't know what to do. I was silenced. My legs began to shake and I just shook my head and felt like I was going to vomit and die and shake myself into convulsions all at once. B.D. passed out the letter to everyone and Elena stared at me like I was some sort of criminal. This was so bizarre that I think I went ahead and had a major panic attack right there in the living room. Alan looked uncomfortable. B.D. read the letter and emphasized the part of the Rilke poem that read "Are there no places on your dear body that keep remembering like eyes." I was in a trap and didn't know what to do. Then B.D. spoke.

"I show you all this letter because it illustrates what happens when we break trust. Simeon broke a contract, a man contract by going after my woman. I spent my time trying to help him, taking him to spiritual places that the big boy didn't know existed and this is how he repays me." Fred the former Porsche salesman was staring at me and shaking his head. I was scared. I didn't know what they were going to do. Alan was fidgeting in his chair. I was embarrassed and not sure if I had done something wrong or not. I looked over at Elena and she looked down. How in the hell did I get myself in this position? Of all the weekends and stupid meetings this was by far the worst scenario of all, and it came about the day I was trying to free myself from the group. Then the tanned bottom feeder spoke.

"It is funny, Simeon, that you should talk about leaving when the reason I brought this letter tonight was to illustrate how much you need to learn. How immature you are. How the only person you care about is yourself and that your selfish interest in Elena was more important than your kindness and respect for me and the rest of the group." Alan's face was turning a shade of red.

"I'm angry at you, Simeon, because you deceptively tried to steal my woman, but also because you betrayed my trust in you. I gave to you. You took from me." Fred was shaking his head and looked like he was ready to kill me. I took a deep breath and tried to collect myself and I looked at the door and tried to figure out some way to escape. I now realized what this was all about. They were trapping me and using Elena to keep me in the fitness cult. They were abusing me and her and Alan and everyone to keep the weekends going, to keep the group intact, so they could fuel their egos and take our money. I looked over at Alan, straight into his eyes and I stood up, all 220 pounds of me, and took a stand.

"Goodbye, B.D., Fred, Elena. You guys are scam artists. All three of you are psychotic and abusive. I loved Elena, and I'm sorry if she was your woman, but that is not what she told me. And, Fred, I think you should go back to selling goddesses or cars or whatever it was you did before you decided to brainwash me." I looked at B.D. like I was going to punch him all the way to Nevada and let him know by the look in my eyes that if he took one step closer to me I would pound him. I cracked my neck in a show of force. Then I turned to my college buddy Alan and said, "Let's go, Alan." And, in the greatest move of his life, he stood up, slowly, but he stood up, and he looked at B.D. with determined eyes and said, "See you later, fake Menehune stripper man." And shaking but elated, we walked out of the incense-filled castle of spiritual abuse and got in the white princess and drove away victorious and proud. Then, five seconds into the drive, my car radio began to work. Slowly and filled with static at first, she turned on. I adjusted the dials and Alan and I drove back into town, in style, the music playing, filled with a drunk silence.

CHAPTER 11

I was so proud of Alan and proud of myself that I didn't want to ruin it by talking. When I got to where Alan lived he turned toward the car door and started opening it. I could tell he felt uncomfortable about the whole evening.

"Alan, I was really proud of you tonight," I said, trying not to be too paternal.

"Thanks, Simeon, I would never have been able to say that or leave without you urging me on. I hope you aren't upset with me for getting you involved with Pure USA. I'm a bit confused right now."

"Alan," I said, "I'm not mad at you in the least bit. I think in some strange way it was good for me to go through all of this."

"You know that they're ex-strippers, don't you?"

"What do you mean?" I asked.

"Elena, B.D. and Fred, they all used to work for the same stripping agent."

"That figures," I said. "How did you find that out?"

"A guy I worked with saw me looking up the web site for the gym and said he recognized Elena and B.D. from a strip club he used to go to called the Meat House. They had guys and girls shows and evidently B.D. kind of ran the whole thing until he got involved with EST and the Dances with Elks Foundation or whatever it's called. I didn't believe him at first but I asked B.D. and he said that he was a lot of things before he became the healer he is today."

"He's not a healer, Alan. You know that, right?" I asked him.

"Yeah. I know. I just feel so stupid for all of this. My parents were right. This whole thing was a joke. No wonder he wanted us to be nude, on the Men-Being-Men Weekend. I'm surprised he didn't make us do a striptease in between yoga poses." He laughed but I could tell there were tears collecting in his eyes. I decided I shouldn't leave him alone, so I asked him if before he went home he wanted to go get some Chinese and talk about things.

"I don't know," he said. "I've been watching what I eat."

"You ever seen a fat Chinese person?" I told him smiling.

"Not in a long time," he said and closed the car door, and we were off to the Chinese Kingdom to eat like two men back from the toils of war.

It was an extra special night at the Kingdom. Chef Chen had gone haywire the week before and the menu, at least the Chef's Specials, were alarmingly inventive. We ordered a Shrimp with Asparagus dish, a Mango Shrimp and a couple of varieties of Lo Mein. I felt whole. I decided that the air was full of closure and I breathed in courage from the Szechuan atmosphere and decided tonight, I would find out not only where they all shower, but what they eat when the customers aren't around. I got up from the table and made my way into the kitchen, slowly, humbly, with my hands behind my back, and I walked straight into my short-haired waitress friend, folding what would eventually become Won Tons and she said, "Can we help you? What do you need? More tea? Beer?"

"No," I said, calm as a koala bear. "I want to know where the showers are?"

"Showers are for employees only," she said a bit aggressively.

"I understand, but I need to know where they are. I'm doing a story on showers in restaurants for a fitness magazine in town, and I wanted to highlight your restaurant because I heard you offer that service to your employees."

"You need to talk to manager. He not here."

"Okay, well, can I set up an appointment to come back and take some pictures of the showers?" The cook started yelling in Chinese just as he was dropping my mango into the pan.

"Well, tell me this, if you don't mind," I said. "How many of the employees at the Kingdom ride their bikes to work?" The chef continued to yell and point to the exit door.

"We all ride bike," she said. "Come Tuesday, manager help you with story."

"Thank you," I said, and strutted back to the table to meet my friend Alan. What a night. I not only left the fitness cult and helped Alan do the same, but I had cracked the mystery of the Chinese showers and bikes. All that was left was to find out what they ate when we weren't around. I would do that Tuesday. Enough for today. Then our dishes arrived and Alan and I exchanged stories from college and beyond, and, for some reason, probably because it required too much energy, we didn't talk about the gym. Maybe they would all go back to the Meat House on some sort of reunion tour. I thought for a second about Elena and her grandma that I assumed lived in Ecuador and I wondered if she knew about the Meat House and about B.D. Elena probably sent her clothes she had designed for the gym, and that was more than enough for an old woman in Ecuador. Then Alan decided to tell me more about Elena and B.D.

"You don't know the whole story about Elena and B.D., do you, Simeon?"

"I guess not," I said. "But why didn't you tell me all this stuff before, Alan?"

"I didn't know what was going on between you guys so I didn't want to interfere," he responded. I couldn't blame him. I didn't really tell him I was in love with Elena.

"About ten years ago, B.D. went to Ecuador with a group of men who decided that going to South America would help them forgive their fathers. I think this was the first of many 'men' trips that B.D. would take. Anyway, he was camping with this group and doing yoga, breathing and chanting and all of that, when an old truck pulled up to the campsite. According to B.D., the men were drunk and stumbling all over the place and one of them had a gun. B.D. and the other men with him looked at each other in fear and then stood up and said hello and tried to be cordial. B.D. noticed a young girl in the cab

147

of the truck with dirt on her face, beaten and crying. He could only imagine what had happened to her. And I guess it was at that point that he got in touch with his life force, because he decided, right then and there, that he would save that girl from these two drunk and angry men. The stumbling men were pissing on the tires of the car and laughing and bumping into things and B.D. just looked at the deep, dark, sad eyes of the girl in the truck and something inside of him urged him to walk up to the truck, put out his hand to the scared girl, help her out of the truck and lead her to stand behind the other four men in his group. They formed a sort of wall, a potential death wall considering one of the drunk guys had a shotgun. The men walked over to B.D. and yelled something in Spanish and pointed at the girl. The man pulled up his shotgun and pointed it at her and then at each of the men individually. B.D. just stared him down, I guess. And then, because the guy was so drunk, he tripped over a rock, fell backwards and the gun went off into the air. The men started laughing and B.D., like a cat, pounced on the man and got the gun."

"Amazing," I said. "How did you find out about all of this?"

"B.D. told me the story a few years ago, and I learned more about it from tutoring Elena in English," he said.

"What do you mean?" I asked.

"The eighteen-year-old girl in the truck was Elena," he said. "One of the men in the truck was her father. B.D. decided he couldn't let her go back to that life so the entire group went into town, found a minister and B.D. married her right there so that she could get out of Ecuador. They paid all the right people and got the papers signed, and, a day before they were supposed to completely forgive their fathers, they flew back to the U.S. with an eighteen-year-old girl who didn't speak a word of English."

"She was eighteen?" I asked.

"Eighteen or nineteen, I'm not sure. He took Elena to live with his mother and sister for three years in Chicago and he sent them money every month to pay for her education and clothes and stuff, and would visit her and his mom and sister on holidays. B.D. and her began as friends, almost like siblings, but then, after about five years, they started falling in love. I think she always saw him as her savior," he said.

"Well he was," I added.

"Elena moved out to California when she was twenty-three and her and B.D. began to live together."

"So, they're married?" I asked.

"They got married in Ecuador," he said, "not here, so I don't know what that means exactly." I started to feel terrible. No wonder she acted so bizarre with me. I felt like a jerk. They were married. I had no idea. The Chinese food began to taste bitter in my mouth and I began to feel sick. I had fallen in love with a married woman, I was just like my dad, chasing after married women, or chasing after women while I was married, however you want to describe it. It's all bad.

"They kind of go back and forth," Alan said.

"What do you mean?"

149

"Sometimes they're like a couple and other times they fight and hang out with other people. They have a strange relationship. I think, because it began as it did, the lines will never be real clear." Little did I know, Alan was a relationship genius.

"That is bizarre," I said, feeling a little bit better but still ready to vomit on command. It all began to make sense to me, no wonder he was so mad at my love letter and the poem and the crushed rose. Uh oh. No wonder he saw her as his possession and no wonder she felt trapped by him. No wonder she hugged and kissed him at the airport. It was all beginning to make sense. And, for a moment, I began to see things as gray. I hate gray. B.D. wasn't evil and I wasn't all good. We were both involved, and in some way, both guilty of the same sin.

I wasn't as talkative and as care-free for the remainder of the meal. Alan was still in shock about leaving the gym and now I wasn't completely sure I handled myself correctly. I know they were all three unhealthy people, but maybe they weren't as bad as I thought. I don't know. I do think it was right to get out of their sick group, but maybe I was a little bit sick, too. I mean, how could I fall in love with Elena so quickly? I think I wanted to save her, too, or have her save me, but from what? I don't know. And why did I want to take her away from B.D.?

I drove Alan home, and, in some strange way, I think he felt much better than I did. He had finally made a decision he was proud of. I guess I saved him, too. I was just wandering around the place trying to save everybody. I was the savior of Santa Barbara, fumbling my way through tractor stories and Greek class, camouflaging my real

150

purpose, which was to snatch people from the throes of entrapment and take them to my safe haven where I would protect them all with my velvet disposition. What a sham. Now I was the sham. I was the fake Shaman. I was the former Porsche salesman. Uh oh. The whole thing was turning upside down on me and now I wasn't sure which way to turn. I got home, turned on some music, sat on my couch and watched cable access television for six hours to numb the pain.

I got up the next morning to make my way into the office. I didn't want to be there. I didn't want to function. My world was upside down. I was so clear twenty-four hours ago. I thought I had been tricked by the stupid Pure USA Gym and B.D. and Fred and Elena. I thought by getting up the courage to leave them all I was making a mature, self-aware decision. But then I found out some new information. My head was filled with images of the two drunk men, Elena sitting in the dirty truck, her eyes, her room with B.D.'s mom, the taste of her lips, her smell, adultery, the Meat House, red Porsches, Alan's parents, showers in Chinese restaurants, rocket launching, Dr. Diesel, spiced ham, the Beatitudes, the stoned anthropology students, my weight issue and the fact that my Grandma was dying of colon cancer. I bought a pack of five-dollar French cigarettes, Gitane Blondes, and decided I wasn't going to make it to work that day. I needed a self-day. I went to a pay phone, lit up a smoke and called Peter. "Man Tractors, this is Peter," he said.

"Peter, this is Sim."

"Hey, Simeon, you're running a little behind schedule. Let me guess, a late evening with your South American princess." He was in a good mood.

"No, not even close," I said. "I kind of need a self-day."

"Well, that is too bad, Sim, because today we are shooting the ad with Rando which will be fun."

More fun for him than me, I thought.

"But do what you need to do and I'll see you tomorrow." he said.

"Thanks, Peter."

"Are you okay, Sim?"

"Not really," I said and I could feel tears well up in my eyes and I couldn't talk any more.

"I care about you a lot, Simeon. You know that, don't you?" Peter said, like a best friend does right when you need it most.

"I do know that, Peter."

"It's Thursday," he said. "Take two days off and work on your stories at home. And call me if you want to talk."

"I will," I said, and hung up and walked around smoking and looking for a hot cup of coffee. It was eight days before my twenty-fourth birthday and I had officially lost my footing. I made my way to get some food and decided I would just go home for a while, until noon, when I could go back out and catch a matinee. I wandered home, smoked like a chimney and drank way too much coffee.

When I got home there was a message from my mom inviting me to come to North Dakota the following weekend for my birthday. Evidently there was some sort of flight deal and my mom had made me a tentative reservation. I felt better. She was worried my grandmother wasn't going to make it much longer, so the trip might be the last time I would see her alive. I called her back and left her a message that I would love to come see her and my grandmother for the weekend and that it was just what I needed. I'm sure she would be able to tell from my voice that things were not going well. Moms can sense things. I sat around and decided to read my journals from Ecuador. I couldn't get the image of Elena in that truck out of my mind. It made me sick.

I awoke this morning and went to the Campo. We all piled into Father Diego's truck and headed to the country. On the way we hit an iguana and veered violently to miss another. The first parish we went to was an open school with goats and dirt all around, sitting at the base of an Andes-like hill covered with fog. It was tropical and lush. People lined up to give confession and then his teaching began. He spoke of confession and that sin is not only something you do, but also the things that you don't do. He told them that God knows human needs and desires and that nothing is a surprise. He told them once they confessed that they were free. His approach was friendly, respectful and honest. He did not threaten or push. The next village we went to had a river running through it and we walked around and bought a Coke. A boy named Mario walked up to me and told me to come look at the grave of his two grandmothers and some other family members. He was eleven years old and very proud of his family and his town. He talked a lot but I didn't understand everything he was saying.

I remembered that boy and the smell of the town and the dirt. He was so proud of the graves. They weren't like our graves, they were right in the middle of town and children would play around them and drop off flowers in the morning on their way to school. It was a much different view of death. We put our relatives in graves on hills outside of town and visit them once a year, if at all. We choose not to think about it, not to recognize them. Anywho. Underneath the journal entry was a scribbled quote from *The Brothers Karamazov* that read,

After a ruthless analysis the scholars of this world have left nothing of what was held sacred before. But they have only investigated the parts, and overlooked the whole, so much so that one cannot help being astonished at their blindness.

I guess I thought that this quote applied to death and graves and things that are held sacred. I'm not sure why it was in my journal but I liked it. I spent the rest of the day trying to get some work done and making a few phone calls for some stories I was working on, but, in the back of my mind I was thinking about Mario, the eleven-year-old boy, and his grandmother, and about my grandmother in North Dakota. When I was younger she used to make these cinnamon rolls that were filled with butter and frosting and nuts and raisins. They are still the best cinnamon rolls I have ever tasted.

That night I went to my Greek class and we struggled over some lines from the *Odyssey* and talked about the difference between New Testament and Homeric Greek. It was interesting but my mind was still thinking about all that had happened the past few days. It became clear to me that I had some growing up to do.

CHAPTER 12

Monday came soon enough and it was a good day at work because it was just Andrew and I. Peter was at meetings all day with masculine men, probably daydreaming about Dr. Diesel, and I got the chance to talk to my mom and firm up the plans for my trip the following weekend. I was supposed to head over to the Chinese Kingdom the following morning, so I gave them a call to make sure they remembered.

"Chinese Kingdom, can I help you?"

"Yeah, hi, this is Simeon. I am the man who wants to take pictures of your showers for a magazine."

"You want order to go?"

"No, I mean maybe later, but right now I just want to know if the owner is in."

"Hello, Chinese Kingdom, can I help you?"

It was a different person.

"Hi, I am Simeon and I want to come down there and take pictures of your shower for an article."

"Yes, Shimeon. Come on down. We are ready for article. See you soon." And he hung up. I guess today was the day. I wasn't feeling that up to it, but I couldn't let an opportunity like this pass me by. Peter was gone. It was almost 10:30, which in some cultures is lunch time, so I told Andrew we were going on a field trip and collected the lights and my camera equipment and we were on our way. I brought an overabundance of equipment, most of which I had no idea how to use, but I wanted to look official. I had been waiting for this to happen for a very long time.

On the way to the restaurant I explained to Andrew that I had this theory about showers and bicycles and Chinese restaurants that had been bothering me for a long time. He didn't think it was odd in the least bit; He said, "You don't have to explain it to me anymore; remember, you're talking to a former obsessive rocket launcher." We laughed, and he helped me carry in all the equipment. The Kingdom looked immaculate. All the staff were standing in a line when we arrived, smiling and happy. I began to feel a little bit guilty. We said hello and took a few preliminary shots of all of them standing together by a sign that said, "We welcome friends and lovers," a bit of a mistranslation probably, but nice nonetheless. You know that is another topic I would like to look into some time. Who translates these things from Chinese to English? I mean, on the front of the menu at the Kingdom there are these beautiful Chinese letters, which obviously represent some sort of poem or something and below it says in English, "We have food for minds alive in Green waterfalls." What does that mean? Anywho, that is another project. We made our way into the spotless kitchen and found the very thing we were looking for, an employee shower, dressing room and hair-dryer connected to the wall. There was a men's room and a women's room.

"For our staff," Chef Chen said and smiled. I couldn't believe it. It was the mother lode. A complete shower back there where they make the Moo Goo Gai Pan. Amazing. I set up some lights and Andrew held a piece of white construction paper to bounce some more light on the shower and we took a few pictures. I decided I was going to get to the bottom of all of this.

"Do you all ride bikes to work?" I asked.

"Yes, all but handsome owner, I drive Mercedes." They laughed. Andrew laughed. "Well, can I take a picture of all of you next to your bikes?" They all smiled and looked at me as if I was crazy.

"Why are you interested in bikes?" the owner asked.

"Well, because they all fit together, you need a shower in here because everyone rides bikes to work, right?"

Like the explosion of a diesel engine firing up, he said, "No. Shower for after work. Before we go home to family. Not for bikes." I was floored. I became dizzy. My theory was shot. There was a world full of people riding their bikes to work and not showering. Maybe they at least washed up a bit, or changed.

"Nice shower, huh?" asked the owner.

"It's gorgeous," Andrew said. I took one more photo of all of them by the shower. Andrew suggested we take a shot of the owner using the hair dryer. I thought it was a little cruel, but he wanted to do it. There he was smiling, blow-drying his hair in front of the staff and thinking in some way this was going to help his business. I shot a few photos, trying not to laugh. We packed up and told them the photo shoot was over.

"When's article coming out?" the owner asked.

"In three months," I said. "I'll show it to you when we get some copies." I was beginning to feel really guilty now, especially about the blow-drying incident. We made our way to the car and Andrew looked like he was on the moon again, driving one of those four-wheel-drive golf carts with big tires.

"That was bizarre," he said. We drove back to the office.

When we got back, there was a message from Peter to page him at his meeting, and I did. He called back a few minutes later and asked me to write some copy for the subscription giveaway featuring Dr. Diesel. He had forgotten to do it and it was due at 3:00. I sat down thinking about the hair-dryer photo, sent Andrew to the lab to get the film we had shot developed and came up with this ad copy. It would be revised later, but not much.

"Why should you subscribe to *Man Tractors*? That is your question. Because we rule. That is our answer. Two hundred pages every month of high-powered tractor action, news, tests, reports, new products and interviews. If you're an American, and you should be, or just an American sympathizer, which everyone is, you need this magazine. You need *Man Tractors*. Get it. And if we can't convince you, maybe the most famous tractor rapper of all time can help you on your way to becoming informed. With every two-year subscription you will receive Dr. Diesel's new album, *Live From The Dirt*. Dr. Diesel says, "If you don't read *Man Tractors*, you ain't a tractor lover. And if you ain't a tractor lover, than you ain't a Dr. Diesel fan. Pretty simple. Enjoy *Man Tractors*."

Peter liked the copy and especially the quote from Rando. The photo Peter chose to run with the copy was of Rando sitting on a tractor with a group of gospel singers flanking him. They were wearing blue and Rando had on all yellow. It was dramatic. The tractor was a green, $250,000 scraper on loan from CAT. If they only knew.

The middle of the week was uneventful except for my classes on Tuesday and Thursday and my feelings of guilt and confusion about the gym and Elena and B.D. I decided it was too complicated to obsess about and I'd let it rest for a while. I would come back and think about it after my birthday. Sometimes you just have to let things filter a bit. So that is what I did.

Andrew got the film developed and we convinced Peter to somehow incorporate the showers and the hair-drying episode into his monthly column, that way I wouldn't feel that bad. I would just tell Chef Chen that we liked the story so much that, instead of giving it to the fitness magazine, we used it. I wasn't sure how he was going to fit that into a tractor magazine but he said he would. I liked Peter very much. He had the uncanny ability to give you a break when you needed it, but without letting you know what he was doing.

Friday was a good day. I was going to fly to North Dakota at around noon, so Peter, Rando and Andrew took me out to breakfast to celebrate my birthday before I left. We went to the International Hut of Waffles, an obvious spin-off of the famous breakfast chain and ate waffles and sausage and bacon and drank way too much coffee. Andrew gave me a book on Russian mystics that he said he really enjoyed, and Peter gave me $100 and a card and told me to take my mom and Father Michael out to a nice dinner. He also gave me a check to give to my mom to help with her home for runaway kids. Sometimes I think Peter is from heaven. I think he grew up in Las Vegas, which, as most people know, is far from heaven, but still, his generosity never ceases.

Rando was a little preoccupied because he was about to fly off as well for a concert in Washington to benefit the wine growers who had their vines damaged by some black fungus. He was versatile. I wondered how the snobby vintners would take to his down-home rapping style. I think he was concerned about that as well. The concert was going to be televised on the National Country Music Channel (NCMC) so Peter and Andrew said they would tape it for me if I couldn't get it in North Dakota.

I made my way to the airport, caught a flight from Santa Barbara to LAX and I was off to Richardton. My mom picked me up in a large van that read "Hope House" and we hugged for a while and she cried and tears welled up in my eyes. It had been too long, over two years, since I had seen her. She looked the same and had twice as much energy as the last time I saw her.

"We have a full house," she said. "Because of the drought we've been experiencing, there are a lot of runaways in Richardton. Parents tend to take things out on their children, which is really sad." We have over twenty guests now, so you're going to have to sleep on the couch, even though it's your birthday."

We drove into town and I felt at peace. She had so much love in her, it's hard to describe, but she was radiant. We talked about Elena a bit and about work and my classes and Andrew and then she said, "It just so happens that I have a young woman working for me now who I am sure you are going to be interested in meeting." I couldn't believe she was trying to set me up.

"I don't want to meet anyone right now, Mom, at least not anyone who lives in North Dakota." In her regular graceful tone she said, "Well, I'm sorry but she lives with me, so I'm sure you'll end up running into her sometime this weekend." My palms began to sweat. It was just like my mom to be working behind the scenes to try to find me a wife. I could feel my body temperature increase by ten degrees.

"Why are you so quiet?" she said. "Thinking about your new friend, Keana?" She was smiling mischievously.

"Is that her name?" I asked.

"Yeah, isn't it a pretty name? She is Native American, Mexican and German. Her parents live in Arizona and she's getting her Master's in Social Work and so as part of her studies she is working with me for a semester. I think you're going to like her."

I was already nervous. "Mom, I was kind of looking forward to a relaxing weekend. There's been a lot going on in my life, I don't really want to get all freaked out right now."

"Why would Keana freak you out? You don't have to like her. I mean, you don't have to fall in love with her, she's going to be very busy all weekend with the kids, so don't worry about it." She was still smiling. Well, at this point I started to feel a little bit better. I was emotionally unavailable. I was nervous to meet her, but not like I usually am. I didn't have the energy.

"Peter gave me some money to take you and Father Michael out to dinner tonight," I said.

"That sounds great, and then tomorrow I'll cook you your favorite dinner for your birthday, or at least something that will be easy to prepare for twenty-four people." It was going to be a big birthday party. My mom and I, this Keana person, Father Michael and twenty runaway children from the Hope House. I was a little bit dizzy. We pulled up to the old Victorian house and I put my stuff in the living room and walked around the place a little bit. There were kids everywhere. My mom introduced me to as many as she could and I could see the anger and the confusion in their eyes. It was time for them to be heading to bed so most of them were busily brushing their teeth or already in their rooms. The upstairs of the house had two huge rooms with ten bunk beds each where they all slept. Once they were all in bed my mom walked up to a room on the left and began to read to them. I don't know why, but I could feel tears well up in my eyes. I listened from outside the door to her voice and the way she overemphasized certain parts of the story, and then I heard another voice coming from the room on my right. I slowly walked over. The door was ajar and so I stood behind it and listened. It was a young, sweet, calm voice. It was Keana.

"And the little boy walked up to the owl and asked him, 'Mr. Owl, why don't you sleep at night? Aren't you tired?' And the owl replied, 'I stay awake, with my big brown eyes to watch over you while you sleep. To protect you from bad dreams and scary thoughts. When you wake up and eat your breakfast and go to school, I rest so I can watch over you when you go to bed again.'"

And I decided, right then and there, that I wanted to meet this Keana.

I went downstairs and waited for my mom to come down so we could go get a late dinner, and I was hoping Keana would walk down the stairs with her and I could meet her. I went into the kitchen and splashed some cold water on my face and grabbed a strong breath mint from my coat pocket and waited. And waited. My mom walked down and grabbed a coat and told me Father Michael couldn't join us for dinner. "Well, maybe Keana would like to join us," I said with a whole lot of charm.

"That would be nice," she said, "but she needs to stay here with the kids. You can meet her tomorrow, if it doesn't freak you out too much. We can go by and see your grandma on the way, I know she would love to see you."

We walked out the door and I started thinking about the name Keana and how it sounded like the Greek word for ocean, Okeanos, that we had just read the previous week. Maybe it was a sign. I had brought my Greek copy of the *Odyssey* with me so I would check it out later.

We drove to where the old people lived who were waiting to die, I think it was called Villa Rosa, to visit my grandmother. I began to think about why we put old people in these places. I guess we are done with them, and they get in the way so we keep them in this sterile unfamiliar environment to waste away. I know most of the time parents or grandchildren can't take care of them anymore and that's why they put them in the group homes, but there must be something else we could do. It's like summer camp for the elderly, only you can never come back home. People send you letters and come and visit you every once and a while, like parent day at summer camp, then they go home and you have to stay, whether you like it or not. It is really sad. It is sad to throw heroes and heroines together in an unfamiliar, sterile setting that smells like lost hope and then make them wait for death to arrive. It makes me sick. Why can't people keep their parents with them in their homes? I asked my mom as we drove up to the Villa Rosa.

"Mom, I don't like these places. Why do families put people they love in these holding tanks? Why don't they just let them stay at home to die?"

"I think it's different for everyone, Sim, but for me, I couldn't take care of your grandma any longer, she required constant medical attention. I visit her every morning and sometimes in the evening, and all her needs are taken care of."

"I still don't like it," I said. "It just seems like in most cases families put their grandparents in here because they're getting in the way."

"I am sure that happens, Sim, but that's not why your grandmother is in here. She is dying of cancer and I was not able to care for her," she said and tears welled up in her eyes. I felt like a jerk.

"I didn't mean to upset you, Mom, I'm sorry." I saw a renegade tear roll down her cheek, determined to make it to the bottom of her chin, and I put my finger on her face and grabbed the tear and looked at it on my finger.

"It's okay, Sim, it's just been really hard to watch her go and to feel responsible for her well being. It's a lot to think about." She took a deep breath.

"I didn't mean to upset you. I know you have her best interest at heart. I was just thinking out loud," I said. I forgot how sensitive she was and how much she loved people and tried to keep hurt away from them. She was a blanket of protection for me and the children at her home and for my grandma. She took another deep breath and we got out of the car and walked in to see my grandma. For a minute I felt like my dad; he probably did and said all kinds of insensitive things to her and maybe that was why she was crying. We walked toward the front door. "Mom, I'm sorry, I know how well you care for grandma and everyone in your life. Can I take it back?" And I hugged her.

"Yes, you can take it back," she said, and we walked into my grandma's room.

Her eyes were closed and machines were blinking and she looked like she only weighed 50 pounds; her hair was thin and her skin was dry and I began to feel sick. Why hadn't I come to see her more often or written to her once a week or something? I wouldn't exist if it wasn't for her and I certainly wouldn't have made it through college or been able to take my classes now if she hadn't been helping me out. I was the problem.

"Mom, guess who's here?" my mom said. "Simeon is here to see you, he came all the way from California." Her eyes opened slowly and she looked at my mom and then at me and cracked a smile. She needed some water and my mom put a straw up to her lips and she drank a little and then said, in a whisper, "You're not missing any meals, are you?"

I smiled. "No, Grandma, I don't remember the last time I missed a meal." I grabbed her hand.

"It shows," she said. We all laughed a little bit. I didn't mind that she thought I was heavy if it made her smile. She always was a little gruff and it actually made me feel better to know she still had her spunk. We stayed with her for a while and I watched my mom pick up things around the room and rearrange the pictures of family members. There were pictures everywhere of me and of my grandpa when he was younger and my mom and various aunts and uncles who had died. Then my grandma spoke.

"The angel was here yesterday," she said.

"What, Mom? I couldn't hear you."

"The angel was here yesterday again."

"I know, she told me she visited you yesterday," my mom said. I was completely confused, but I wasn't sure if I should ask about the angel or if it was a little game they were playing about dying or something, so I didn't respond. Then my grandma got me involved. "Have you met the angel, Simeon Stylos?" I shot a glance at my mom to help me, but she just smiled and I looked at my grandma and nervously said, "Which angel is that Grandma?"

"The one that lives with your mother," she said. I still wasn't sure what she meant. My mom jumped in. "He hasn't met her, but I think he heard her," she said smiling. I was confused. I wasn't sure if they were playing a joke on me or what, so I just sat there and smiled.

"Wait until you see her eyes, Simeon, they are deep and brown and radiant," my grandma whispered. Now I really wasn't sure what was going on. And then it was revealed.

"And her name, Simeon," my grandma said. "Her name is the most beautiful I have ever heard: Keana." I just sat there stunned. I thought they were talking about a guardian angel or the angels that old people see before they are going to die, not Keana the reader.

"I believe Simeon wanted her to go to dinner with us tonight, Mom." They were both smiling.

"Dinner with an angel," my grandma said. "Not a bad way to spend an evening." I decided to participate.

"No it wouldn't be," I said. "So is she pretty?" I asked my grandma, holding her hand again.

"No, she's not pretty, Simeon, she's angelic. There's a difference."

"What exactly is the difference?" I asked her.

She took a deep breath, like she was in pain, and then spoke. "Humans are pretty, angels are beautiful, that is the difference." She smiled at me and squeezed my hand and closed her eyes.

My mom walked over to her and put her hands through her thin hair, and said, "You rest now, Mom. Simeon and I will come back tomorrow." I let go of her hand and kissed her on the cheek and we picked up our coats and tucked her in for the night.

My mom was smiling all the way to the car. I took the keys from her and opened her door and we drove away from the Villa Rosa to downtown to get some dinner. Richardton is not an epicurean's paradise, but my mom knew of a diner called Jack's that was open late, so we made our way there, found a booth and ordered some food. I was hungry. My mom knew everyone in the restaurant including the waiter and the bus-boy and introduced me to them all. I could barely get a piece of steak in my mouth before another person would come by and say, "Good evening, Mary, this must be Simeon, all grown up and done with college." I would stand up and shake their hand and my mom would describe how it was my birthday the following day and how we had just seen my grandma and how I was a writer in California for a tractor magazine and on and on. Then they would smile, genuinely, and say goodbye and welcome home and stuff like that. It was nice the first few times but then it began to bother me. I was hungry. We were having a nice time, though; it had been a while since I shared a meal with my mom and I forgot how graceful and kind she was. It made me feel like I had a chance to become like her.

My back was to the door but I could hear the phone ring and the waiter pick it up and say, "Jack's" and then he called for my mom to come to the phone. I watched her walk over to the phone, gracefully, not nervous, not agitated, resigned. She looked concerned on the phone, and she walked back and said, "Sim, I'm sorry, but we have to go. Two new kids came to Hope House and Keana is having hot chocolate with them, but they need some medical help and I need to tend to them." I could see tears in her eyes. She hadn't even met them, and already she was crying for them. I was so overcome by her compassion. We stood up and I paid for the meal and the waiter hurried as if this happened periodically, and we got in the car and rushed home.

CHAPTER 13

We walked in the front door and my mom asked me to wait in the living room while she went into the kitchen to meet the kids, and let them know they were welcome and loved and she would do everything she could to help them.

She called a doctor and Father Michael. It had been a strange evening. A part of me wanted to get a look at Keana, but then I felt terribly guilty for thinking about that when there were hurt children in the room with her, so I just sat down on the couch and prayed for the first time in a while. I asked God to give the children peace and to heal their wounds and to give my mom the courage to help them.

I sat there in silence in the dark until Father Michael and the doctor walked in the front door. I stood up and walked over to them and Father Michael looked at me and said, "You must be Simeon. I feel like I know you. Your mom talks about you very often. She is so proud of you."

I liked him instantly. He looked at me with a sad grin and said, "Excuse me for a minute. I need to help your mom."

I let go of his hand and took a step back and watched him and the doctor I didn't meet walk in through the swinging kitchen door. I knew he was a Jesuit priest and he helped my mom with the Hope House and they had become good friends, but that's all I knew about him. He was handsome and had piercing eyes. What is it with all these eyes lately? It seemed like my life was suddenly filled up with them.

I waited in the living room for a while and then sat down on the couch. I was so tired from the trip that when I closed my eyes I fell asleep for a moment. I woke up a few minutes later because my mom was tapping my shoulder and saying, "Simeon, there are some people here I want you to meet."

Oh God. It was time for Keana the reader and here I was asleep and groggy and not ready. I followed my mom into the kitchen as she walked up to two children, a boy around ten years old and a girl around seven.

"This is my only son, Simeon. He is staying with us for the weekend. Simeon, this is Clare and Thomas." I didn't know if I should shake their hands or hug them, so I just crouched down next to their chairs and said hello. I couldn't believe their eyes. Just my luck. Both of them, brother and sister, had deep blue eyes, red now because of the crying, wet with tears. An aunt had brought them to Hope House after she found them at home, beaten and crying. My mom touched them both often, tenderly, while she told them how

171

much they were going to enjoy staying with all of us. She told them they were going to stay for a while until they felt better. Father Michael was on the phone in the other room filing a report with Social Services and explaining the situation.

My mom had a special room in the house for first-time visitors. It was a comfortable and warm and hopeful room with clouds painted on the ceiling. There were dozens of teddy bears and toys and two inviting beds. She said it was time for them to go to bed and I told them goodnight. I watched my mom hold their hands and she said, "Sim. I'll stay with Thomas and Clare until they fall asleep, so why don't you grab some blankets and go to bed on the couch? I'll see you in the morning." They walked upstairs and I went to the couch. As I was falling asleep I was thinking about their eyes and about what would have happened to them if the Hope House didn't exist. I felt sick, thinking about the vulnerability of children, and I didn't sleep very well.

When I woke up, I felt a tingling in my stomach that reminded me it was my birthday. The day I was born, twenty-four years ago. My parents only son, Simeon. The kids were getting up all over the house and the air was filled with the buzz of children getting ready for the day. Today was Saturday, parent visitation day, so the children were getting ready, in most cases, to see the people responsible for their stay at the Hope House. I listened to kids slam doors, sing in the shower, yell at each other to hurry up, slam more doors, and then saw, with my own two eyes, the second most beautiful girl in the world, Keana. She was about five foot six, with olive skin, brown eyes, dark, long hair and she had on light blue overalls and funky shoes. I could sense her confidence. I fell apart.

"Good morning, Simeon," she said. "I'm Keana."

My palms turned warm instantly. I shook her hand.

"Hi, Keana, it's nice to meet you." She had beautiful teeth and a great smile. I took in a deep breath and came away with a subtle yet charming scent of orange blossoms.

"Your mom has told me all about you," she said.

"Likewise," I blurted.

"Well, I have to get the kids ready for their visitation so I'll talk to you later." I just stared blankly at her.

"Okay. Great. I'll talk to you later." That was interesting. That tingling feeling in my stomach I had when I woke up was aggravated significantly. Keana. Okeanos: The river that began in the underworld and flowed in a circular stream around the earth. That's what the Greeks thought, because they thought the world was flat. Odysseus had to cross the river on his way to Hades to find out how he could safely return home from his journey. We learned that in class. Either way, I loved her name.

I spent most of the day wandering around Richardton, while my mom and Keana were busy coordinating the parental visits. In the afternoon I returned from my sojourn to the smell of tri-tip barbecue in the air. That was my favorite meal and my mom was cooking it for my birthday celebration. I felt like I had come home. I really missed my mom and my grandma and the whole Ecuadorian harlot thing had shown me how important trust and family and true relationships really are. The rest of the day and evening we spent around the house, eating, and the kids got together and sang "Happy Birthday" to me and I opened a few presents from my mom, mostly sweaters, and then my mom told me about a trip we needed to take that evening.

"I wish we could do this tomorrow, Sim, seeing as it's your birthday, but your flight leaves so early, I don't think we will have time." I think she had other motives.

"That's okay," I said. "Where are we going?"

"Well, Keana has an older aunt who lives fifty miles from here on a reservation. She has this herbal mixture formula that's hundreds of years old that supposedly has rid people of cancer. She won't sell it or bottle it, and you have to know her in order to get it, but I thought it would be worth a try for your grandmother. Keana has volunteered to go. Would you mind driving with her? I need to stay here with the kids and I don't want her driving alone."

"That's fine, I could use a little drive," I said. Once the kids were in bed we got into an old Chevy truck my mom had picked up and Keana and I pulled out of the driveway into the still North Dakota night.

The strange thing about the whole ride was not the actual mission to find some healing herbs for my grandmother—it was that I wasn't the least bit nervous around Keana. I felt like I knew her, like I had grown up with her and so we had this history behind us that broke down the normal barriers. She was sitting next to me, the river of love that began in the underworld, and I was driving the most manly of machines, besides a tractor of course, and I felt good.

"So you write for a magazine?" the river asked.

"Yeah, I write for *Man Tractors.*

"Your mom has shown me some of your articles," she said. "You're a good writer."

"Thanks, it's fun," I said. And then the cork popped.

"I hope to write something else, someday, I mean, something that doesn't necessarily have to do with tractors and farmers and things of that nature. I'm interested in a lot of other things, but this is my first job out of college and I'm getting a lot of writing experience."

"That's great," she said. "What do you want to write?"

Oh great. Now I had to come up with something fast.

"I would like to write plays or short stories or something like that."

"I've always wanted to write," she said, "but I don't really have the ability. I don't think like that."

I didn't know what to say next, but I didn't care. I just smiled at her and kept driving down the interstate, happy as a lark. I wanted to pull over, buy a house, get her something formal to wear and make her dinner for the rest of my life.

"I'm graduating this coming fall so I've been thinking a lot about what I want to do," she said.

"That doesn't end, you know."

"What doesn't end?" she asked.

"Thinking about what you want to do with your life."

"Oh, yeah, I know. I do want to work with children, like your mom. She's been a real inspiration to me. The way she treats every child like a blessing, no matter what has happened to them."

"She is amazing," I said. I glanced at her jeans-encased legs. Over the years they would change, get bigger or wider or whatever, but I had a feeling I would still like them. I wasn't thinking about the Ecuadorian princess one bit. I didn't feel the obsessive need to make conversation. I was comfortable. We drove on and eventually came the entrance of the reservation. Keana told me more about our mission.

"This potion or whatever you want to call it has healed many people in my family. My aunt Gia knows we're coming but she might want to talk with us for a while, because I haven't seen her since I was a little girl. I'm not sure." I couldn't believe I was manning a truck in the middle of North Dakota with an angel named after a mythical river at my side going to meet a Native American herbologist by the name of Gia. Earth. But in some weird way it all seemed to make sense.

We parked in front of what looked like an old bus, converted into a permanent residence. We went around back and Keana called her name. "Gia. Hello." I could smell the sweet scent of sage in the air. She called again, "Gia, are you here?" A tiny voice answered from somewhere in the bus. "Keana, is that you? Come in." We walked through the gutted-out bus and found her cousin sitting at a small table in the back of the rig, where the restrooms usually are. There were candles everywhere, and "The Price is Right" was on the television, although the volume was turned off. "It's been too long," Earth said. "And who have you brought with you?"

"This is my friend, Simeon. He is the grandson of the woman I want to help."

"Simeon," she said. "That is an ancient name. Sit down, let me take a look at you."

I sat on a patio chair covered with a blanket and looked at her wrinkled skin and her bad teeth; she stared into my eyes and smiled. "Boy, you have quite a story to tell, don't you, Simeon?"

"I'm not sure," I said. Keana was standing behind me and she put her hands on my shoulders as if to tell me it would be all right. I loved her hands on my shoulders. I could feel her skin through my new birthday sweater. I began to think romantic thoughts about her. Bad timing.

"Your eyes tell a sad story, Simeon. But it has a good ending. A very good ending." She wanted to tell me more but she just smiled and went back into the little closet that used to be the relief station for cross-country bus travelers and came out with a small burlap sack that fit in the palm of her hand. It was tied with thin rope and decorated with Mexican sage. "This is for your grandmother, I hope it isn't too late." She handed the bag to me and then put her hands on my forearm and looked straight into my eyes and smiled again. "Now, Mr. Ancient Eyes, why don't you wait outside for a few minutes while I talk with my long lost Keana?"

I got up and found my way to the opening of the bus and stood outside in the calm night. I walked around with the healing potion in my hand and listened to the coyotes howl and the dogs romping in the yards around Earth's bus. I wanted to know what they were talking about in there, but I was glad to be out of the bus for a minute. I wondered what she meant by my ancient name and my ancient eyes, but maybe that was just her way of being kind to me. I thought about Keana's hands on my shoulders and I was determined to put myself in a situation again that would prompt her to touch me. She had a warm, kind touch, topped off with a good healthy dose of sexuality.

What a birthday I was having. I was on a reservation outside a converted bus, holding a burlap sack of healing herbs, I had been told I had ancient eyes, was touched by an ancient river and fed my favorite meal by my favorite person in the world. Who knew North Dakota was this inspiring? People would move here if this sort of thing happened all the time. I walked down the road a little so as to not look too anxious, and then Keana slowly walked out towards me. She was radiant. She was almost glowing. I wished I was holding a love potion in my hand and could take a sip and give her some and move into the bus with Earth and live there forever. "Are you ready, Mr. Ancient Eyes?" she asked with a smile.

"I am," I said, and I fired up the truck. We pulled out of the reservation onto a lonely, dark road.

The truck was making a strange noise and Keana turned down the radio to listen to the engine. The noise was getting louder. "Pull over, Simeon, I think I know what's wrong." I couldn't believe it. She knows how to fix trucks. I wasn't sure if I should pretend I knew what was going on or not. I thought about mentioning the water pump or the piston rods or alternator or something like that, but I decided to remain quiet. She grabbed a flashlight from behind the seat and I popped the hood. She got up on the bumper for better leverage and was looking at the engine. I wandered around the front of the truck, pretending to be disinterested. "I think it's the fan belt. This has happened before." She got out some tools from behind the seat, and a rag, and began to do something to the fan belt while I held the flashlight.

The thought of some drunk driving by us and seeing Keana fixing the truck while I held the flashlight entered my mind. What would I tell them? "Oh yeah, my woman and I were just picking up some potion from the little lady on the reservation and the fan belt blew and she's got smaller hands than mine so she's fixin'-it." I rehearsed that a few times in my mind, and, when I was done, the belt was fixed and I shut the hood. She wiped off her hands with the rag and said, "Let's go." I got in the truck, fired it up and the noise was gone.

"That was great, Keana. How did you learn to do that?"

"My dad taught me when I was little. We used to have a truck just like this." I was falling for her. Not only was she beautiful, but she could fix a truck on the fly, something that would come in handy if we ended up together, considering I had a hell of a time learning how to put the key in the ignition. "You're not real mechanical, are you, Simeon?"

"No, not really." I said.

"Well, you can write and I can't, so I guess we're even," she said. Even? I was under the impression she was up a few points on me, but if she didn't think so, it was all right with me.

We spent the rest of the drive talking about her parents and her friends and about Peter and Andrew and my job and Dr. Diesel and my Greek classes and more about my mom. It was a nice drive, spent with an amazing woman, the river, Keana, and it was the best birthday I could remember. That night, after Keana went to bed, I looked up the meaning of her name and re-read the part of the *Odyssey* when Odysseus visits Hades and talks with people who have died.

We were going to visit my grandmother in the morning a few hours before my plane took off to Santa Barbara. As it turned out, we were too late.

The phone rang a few times in the middle of the night while I was asleep in the house, but my mom had told me that often the parents of the kids staying at her house would get drunk and call the house saying they were going to take their kids back, so I didn't think anything of it. But at around 4:00 a.m. the phone rang and I could hear my mom talking from upstairs, and I had a sad feeling in my stomach. My grandma had died and the night nurse found her lying in her bed, with her hands folded as if she was praying. My mom came downstairs with tears in her eyes and I was already sitting up ready for her. I hugged her while she cried. I began to cry as well. She said, "I think she waited for you to come here so she could say goodbye."

"Maybe, Mom," I said.

"I hope I did everything I could to help her."

"You did, Mom, you were the best daughter a mom could ever wish for." We sat there for a few moments in the dark, thinking about my grandma, and then we got dressed and went to see her for one last time. My mom was silent as we drove, a woman so surrounded by pain and broken lives, stifled by the pain of death. I wished I could comfort her and make her feel better, but I knew the pain she was feeling was that of a daughter losing a mother and nothing I could say would penetrate that bond. I tried to be strong.

We walked into the Villa Rosa and met with the nurse and my mom hugged her and we walked into her room. She was still lying there, lifeless, her hands folded across her chest. My mom bent down and kissed her and touched her cheeks and looked at her for a moment and then said, "I love you Mom." She broke down and fell to her knees as she held her hand and I walked over and held her hand while she cried. It was difficult for me to see my mom so sad, so broken, in the pose of a daughter, not a mother.

I kissed my grandma and then touched her hand and walked out of the room for a moment to give my mom some time with her. I was crying. Nothing can prepare you for the death of someone you love. The knowledge that it will happen to all of us someday doesn't help a bit. Her skin was old and wrinkled and I know she had lived a full life, but none of that mattered now. I know it didn't matter to my mom. I stood outside the door and imagined my mom in a new dress, ready to start the first grade and then in another dress for junior high. I thought about the love my grandma had shown her when my dad left her to raise me alone. I thought about the look on my grandma's face in the delivery room when she took me from my mom's arms. I know how much my mom loved her and it made me so sad. They were cohorts, partners in life; through the good and the bad they stuck together. My grandma had been helping my mom keep the Hope House open since she started it. I sat down outside the room, closed my eyes and prayed that my grandma was in heaven with the rest of the good people who die every day.

My mom was with her for over an hour, and I sat and waited patiently. When she walked out, she smiled at me, her eyes full of tears. "It was a long goodbye, Simeon. I am so glad you are here with me. I don't think I could have done this without you."

I couldn't believe she found some way through all her pain to make me feel loved. That was her gift, I suppose, and I think she learned it from my grandma.

We walked up to the nurse's office and sat down and my mom filled out some papers and scheduled the cremation that would take place the following day. My grandma didn't want to have a funeral— she thought it was vain—and so my mom respected her wishes, but asked me if I could write something to be read at the service or to be put in the *Richardton Daily* the following day.

"Mom, I can stay until tomorrow or Tuesday and help you. I don't have to go home today."

"No, Simeon, I can handle it alone. You go back home to your life and your job. I'm just so thankful that you were here with me this weekend. It reminds me there is a loving God, a God who knows when people need help." I wanted to stay, but I think in some way she wanted the final goodbye to be between her and her mom. The partners. I had a few hours before I needed to go to the airport and I went outside and sat down on the porch and wrote her eulogy. I decided to write it in the form of a letter to her from my mom and me.

Dear Grandma. This is the last letter I will ever get to write to you, and as often happens, it is a day too late. So, as I write, I'm conscious of the fact that this letter is more for me and Mom and your friends than it is for you. I hope, however, as you sit in your graceful chair in Heaven, you will hear all the people reading about your life, an exemplary life that touched the hearts of all who knew you, and you will smile.

You were a wonderful daughter to your parents, a woman that put herself through school and became an English teacher at Richardton Community College. You were an amazing wife, mother and friend. There are countless people in this community who were helped by your generosity and kindness.

I write you this letter to say thank you. Thank you for your courage, your wit, your ability to tell it like it is, your love of scotch, cards and mystery novels. Thank you for picking me up from school when my mom couldn't. Thank you for your cinnamon rolls that were always hot and full of butter. Thank you for your help, always, and without strings attached, and for your smile. Thank you for being the matchmaker of Richardton, you must be responsible in some subtle yet determined way, for half of the marriages in this town. Thank you for your life, Grandma, and for your faith, and for the peace you spread to all who knew you. I'm sorry you are gone and the world will be less because of your passing. But, I know right now, you are organizing a poker game in heaven, you've sent someone out to get some good scotch and some ice. I wish you peace in your game. Thank you for your life that was shared by many. I love you. Your grandson, Simeon Stylos.

I handed the finished copy to my mom and she read it with tears in her eyes. "It's perfect," she said, then she broke down again. I held her in my arms and wanted so badly to take the pain away from her. We sat down in the living room and talked about my grandma and her life for a few moments, and, when my mom stopped crying, we walked into the kitchen. We had a bite to eat and she told me Keana wanted to take me to the airport. I had forgotten to talk to my mom about the cancer potion so I decided to bring it up. "Mom, I have that potion from Gia, Keana's aunt. Do you want to keep it here with you?"

"No, Sim, why don't you take it home with you and keep it safe? It will remind you of your trip with Keana and of Grandma and of how precious life is."

"Are you sure?"

"Yes, Sim, I'm sure. Give me a big hug and hit the road so you won't miss your flight." She looked like my grandma's daughter when she said goodbye. I pictured her again in her new dress for school, standing on the porch, and it brought tears to my eyes.

I hugged her for a long time and told her to tell Father Michael I said goodbye. Keana came down the stairs with the keys to the truck in her hands. "Are you ready, Mr. Ancient Eyes?" she asked kindly.

"I am." I got into the truck and said goodbye to my mom and to my grandma with a kiss on my mother's cheek. I would miss her very much. I had put the healing potion in my carry-on bag so it wouldn't get crushed. I drove the truck again, with Keana at my side. We talked the whole way to the tiny airport and I asked Keana if I could call her or write to her when I got home. "I would like that, Simeon," she said. I found out she would be returning to the University of Arizona in a month and I mentioned that Arizona was pretty close to California and on and on. I really liked her. In a normal sort of way. It had been a sad weekend, a life-changing few days.

When we got to the airport I went to open my door and she grabbed my hand and our faces headed toward each other in a romantic race. I kissed her, holding on to her hand. It was a short kiss, but one that felt like the beginning of something real. I pulled back and looked into her eyes, calmly, and I smiled and said goodbye. Maybe she pulled me to her because she loved my mom, or because she knew a kiss would dull my pain.

I walked to my terminal and had to wait for a while so I sat down, happy and sad all at once, and thought about the weekend. It was so hard not to give up, give in, see life as a pointless race to the end watching my grandma die. When I saw the pain my mom was going through it made me think of how all the memories, all the parties, weddings, births, baptisms, laughter and accomplishments, fade when someone you love leaves Earth forever. Or maybe it's those very memories that form a blanket of courage to hold you together when someone you love dies. Maybe something as simple as a stolen kiss does make a difference. I don't know, but I want to. I got on the plane thinking about stories that end and stories that begin.

CHAPTER 14

When I got back to work Monday morning I told Peter and Andrew what had happened over the weekend. I told them all about the Hope House and my grandma telling me about the angel and about the mission to get the potion and about how my grandma died with her hands folded on her chest. Peter was a good listener, as was Andrew. They let me alone most of the day, but I did have a story due the following day, so I gathered my thoughts and started writing.

His name is Jacob Jensen. Right now, as you read this story, he is sitting in the Jupiter County jail, eating corn meal and meatloaf, waiting for his day in court. He has probably lost some weight. Chaplains have been visiting him and he has befriended quite a few of the local good ol' boys whose drinking brought them to the attention of the local authorities.

He considers himself a rebel, a modern-day anarchist. He is accused of stealing three sugar cane huskers, four trucks and a small lawnmower from three local sugar cane farmers and driving them straight into Lake Okeechobee. When asked by local reporters why he had done it, he said emphatically, "Sugar kills." When asked what he meant by that, he replied, "Sugar cane kills, just ask Mama." And that was all he had to say on the subject. We tried to contact his relatives, but evidently he is the last surviving Jensen in the area. It's sad to hear about a man gone mad. It's sad to know he is spending his time wasting away in a jail cell, where he will apparently be for the foreseeable future.

However, there's something even more tragic than the plight of Jake Jensen. Under millions of gallons of murky water are eight big machines, eight big manly machines. Never again will they do the work for which they were created, the rough, tough, hard work of shearing off and separating the stalks of the tough sugar cane. Never again will a man climb up, place himself behind the controls and fire up the magnificent creation to fulfill its life's purpose. They are rusting away, their oil and gas seeping into the water and their tires being nibbled on by large freshwater trout. That's the tragedy. Man and machinery are rotting away down in Florida. The man can be punished, rehabilitated possibly, but the machines are lost forever: A tragedy that can never be reversed.

The Jupiter County sheriff sent me some pictures of the aforementioned machines lying on the bottom of the river, and a hilarious one of Jake Jensen flipping off the camera from his cell. It was an interesting story and Peter liked it. The magazine needed some human elements thrown in with all the machines.

We sat around and talked about photos for the upcoming issue and Andrew brought out the shots I had taken at the Chinese Kingdom. We laughed and Peter told us he had written the restaurant into his column on biotechnology by talking about all the vegetables and the tofu that's used in the cooking of Chinese food. He didn't use the shot of the owner with the hair-dryer. Andrew was sad about that. We decided to bring them some of the photos of the group and present them at lunch, which I had decided would lead up to me asking them what they eat when we're not around. I was excited. We made our way to the Kingdom and talked about Rando's concert in Washington and we decided after lunch we would watch the video of Dr. Diesel and the wine growers at the office. We had started to sit at the table when Chef Chen came up and asked, "Is article finished?"

So I stood up and presented him with a picture of the entire staff in the kitchen next to the shower.

"I'm handsome cowboy," he said.

"Yes, you're a handsome cowboy," Andrew responded.

They were all happy with the picture and we ordered some new dishes, an orange and garlic chicken and some asparagus chicken. They were both delightful. Once I was filled with food I mustered up the courage to ask our shorthaired waitress the million-dollar question.

"We were wondering what you guys eat when you sit down together at around three o'clock?"

"What we eat?" she asked.

"Yes, what you all eat every day."

"Oh, Chinese food," she said.

"Yes, I know it's Chinese food, but what dishes exactly do you eat? Are they the same as the ones we eat?" I asked. I was nervous. I was about to discover an ancient truth.

"No, it's different every day."

I had reached a roadblock.

"Well, for instance, what will you eat today?"

"Today?" she asked.

"Yes, today," I replied.

"Too early to eat today. Only Americans eat this early. We eat later. When customers are gone."

She walked away. Andrew looked at me with concern. Foiled again, I thought. She wasn't going to give up the information, even though we gave her a great picture, a picture I was convinced would be framed and put over the front counter with a mistranslation under it like, "Food for the holy and the small, The Chinese Kingdom. We do it for lovers." Or something like that.

We left the Kingdom and I felt a little let down, but all in all I had discovered many things from that little restaurant. When we got back from the restaurant we brewed some coffee and Peter put in the video of Dr. Diesel's show in Washington. He came on after three country bands, so the crowd was shocked by his loud outfit—a silver sequined pair of overalls, gold-painted cowboy boots and a cowboy hat encircled with battery-operated Christmas lights. His D.J. was outfitted in a similar manner and the bass was thumping and he was jumping around. He began to clap his hands and talk in a rhythmic fashion about wine and wine vines and farming and dirt and water and fertilizer and such.

The crowd wasn't getting it. They never got it. He did three songs and decided that he should end the set early. Peter felt bad for him. I guess Rando had called him, upset, after the show and blurted out something about wine growers not having any rhythm and on and on. That happens to artists every now and again; people just don't get their art. Andrew had a funny look on his face while we were

189

watching the video. I think he wanted to feel bad for Dr. Diesel, but he was struck by the humor of the situation. Well, wine growers are a different breed, one that Rando probably shouldn't rap to.

The rest of the week was slow and a little bit sad as I thought about my mom and my grandma. I called my mom that Tuesday and she told me my letter had been published in the Richardton newspaper and people had been calling her and bringing over food. She sounded good, but a little sad.

Then she asked me about my father. She hadn't mentioned him in a long time and I was surprised she did now. She wanted to know if I could call him and let him know that my grandma had died. Apparently he had always been close to my grandma. My mom thought, out of respect, he should know what had happened.

"I don't have his phone number, Mom," I said. "In fact, I don't think he even has a phone. He's still hiding from the Pink Elephant Commission."

"Well, I'll contact his brother and find out where he is, and maybe you can go and see him."

I didn't want to see him and was pretty sure she wouldn't be able to find out where he was anyway, so I just humored her.

"You should try to mend things with him anyway, Sim," she said. "Nothing is worse than carrying around a lot of pain for the rest of your life."

I wanted to remind her she had done it somewhat successfully, but, considering what had happened over the weekend, I let it go.

I began to read the book Andrew gave me for my birthday on Russian mystics, which was interesting. It was a nice break from Greek but, in a strange way, similar. I was fascinated by the way Russia had been converted to Christianity. In the tenth century, Prince Vladimir of Kiev sent emissaries to all parts of the world in search of a religion suitable for his people. The were unimpressed by Western Christianity, which they came across in Germany, decided that Judaism would not suit the Russian temperament, and rejected Islam as soon as they heard of the prohibition on alcohol. Then they attended a liturgy at Agha Sophia in Constantinople. They were moved by the liturgy and introduced Byzantine law and the faith to the people of Russia. Pockets of mystics eventually formed. Many lived primitively, in the mountains, and others lived in the arid desert regions of the Mongolian steppes. I was interested in all of it, but mostly in the fact that young Andrew found peace in these Russian "streltsi," or spiritual fathers. He told me later that week that his letter writing began when he read how these mystics would receive letters from people asking for spiritual and practical advice. He was an interesting bird.

I was thinking about my dad again, probably because my mom had planted the seed, and then she called me with his whereabouts. "I heard from his brother that he's living in a trailer park in Napa Valley called the Trailer Mountain Park."

She told me he had been living there for a few months and that I should see him as soon as possible because he was always on the move. He didn't have a phone, so I couldn't call him. I was nervous and sad. I really didn't want to see him. It had been so long and I didn't know what to expect. I temporarily decided I wasn't going to go to Napa—That is, until I talked about it with Andrew, the former funny farm inmate.

I told him all about my dad and what had happened and how my mom wanted me to tell him about my grandma's death. I also told him how my dad drank too much and had a temper and was on the lam and he was hurtful and immature.

"He is your dad, Simeon, and he deserves to know about your grandma. I wish I could talk to my dad again. I'd give anything to know more about him, even if it was bad. I never got that chance. I don't think you should pass it up."

Andrew's dad had died when he was in the nuthouse. He had been estranged from Andrew and his mother for almost five years.

"I know I'm young and you know more than I do, but I wish I could have your chance again."

He got me thinking. I went home and thought about it for a long time and decided I would be a man, be different than my dad, be better than him and make the effort.

I don't think I could have done it if Andrew hadn't convinced me to take the risk—or if he hadn't asked me where I got the name Simeon.

"It's an odd name," he said. "Your parents must have had a reason for naming you that."

I called my mom that night and she told me my dad insisted on the name, but never really told her why. I think she wanted me to find out from him. I got in my car that Friday after work and reluctantly began the journey to the trailer park where my dad lived. I was nervous. I wished my radio was working because I needed some distraction. I rolled down the window, rested my arm outside the door and felt the friendly wind. So many thoughts went through my mind on that drive. I wasn't even three hours into the drive before I began to feel tears well up in my eyes. I was not convinced this was a good idea, but I continued to drive right up into the heart of California on I-5.

I started to daydream and think about Telemachus, the weak son of Odysseus, who, after years of watching his father's kingdom unravel and his mother being pursued by abusive suitors, set out to find his dad and bring him back home to save his mom and his kingdom. Odysseus was trying to get home with his crew after the Trojan War, but the anger of the sea god Poseidon had kept him away from Ithaca. He spent years trying to get home, but storms, bandits, wars and various adventures prevented his return. I suppose that's a sympathetic reading of the story. He also spent many pleasure-filled evenings in erotic adventures with sea-nymphs and dallied with the gift of immortality. Meanwhile, his wife Penelope was at home fending off the advances of would-be suitors who claimed her husband had been dead for years. She refused to believe it. I wonder if my mom refuses to believe my dad is gone forever. Even though her life is so much better now, I wonder if she, in some way, is still waiting for my dad to come home.

I guess I'm Telemachus, hearing rumors about my dad's whereabouts, hunting him down to bring him back home and save my mom from his enemies. It's the Telemachus Syndrome. I've seen countless actual and would-be therapists on late-night talk shows claim that in all divorced families the only thing the kids want is to somehow bring their parents back together. I'm not sure that's always the case, and, it isn't the case with me. I want to at least know why he doesn't love her anymore, or even care about her, for that matter.

By the time I got up into northern California I had perspired so much I had to change my undershirt at the freeway gas station when I filled up my Swedish Meatball for the last time. It was evening now, clouds were creeping over the mountains and the lights of oncoming cars were beginning to mesmerize me. What was I doing? I was vulnerable. I tried to think about Keana, the river, to give me strength.

I had picked up a map at the gas station that showed most of the landmarks in Napa, mostly wineries, but no trailer parks. What was my dad doing living in a trailer park, anyway? He had once lived in a nice house, had nice cars, was a successful eye doctor, but no more. I know the Pink Elephant Commission was after him, but you'd think he would leave the country, get a small apartment in Paris and paint or something. That's sure as hell what I would do if I had half the population of the western United States after me. I guess we're different.

Once I got into Napa I stopped at a restaurant and asked a woman behind the counter if she knew where the Trailer Mountain Park was located.

"Why do you want to go there?" she asked.

Irritated, I was about to tell her it was none of her business, but I knew that wouldn't be the best way to get her to give me directions. So I just replied, "I've a friend living there, he's a famous poet." I figured that would stir something up.

"Oh, well, that place is a little dangerous. The city's been trying to shut it down for years. Mostly ex-cons and drug dealers live there."

Great. My dad was hiding from the Pink Elephant Commission in a place full of candidates for *America's Most Wanted*. She told me it was a few miles up the road in the foothills of a mountain range.

"Be careful," she said.

"I will."

I drove into the night, scared and confused. I felt like I was picking up my prom date or on my way to the doctor's office to find out some devastating test results. I drove slowly and began to shake. My hands were having a hard time steering the car. I felt like I was three years old again. I tried to breathe deeply for strength but it wasn't working. And then I saw the entrance.

The Trailer Mountain Park was encircled by a large, rusted-out, wrought iron gate draped with different colored Christmas lights. There were dogs and cats everywhere. Most of the trailers were permanent, sadly stationed next to hook-ups and mostly green and

195

yellow. I walked into an office that smelled like chili and saw the legs and one arm of a fat man wearing what looked like sweat pants that were baggy and dirty. I could hear the phony moans, groans and other noises that are a pornographer's idea of sex coming from a television. I was in hell. I rang the bell. He didn't get up. I started out the door when I heard the man turn down the volume of the sex sounds; his chair creaked under all his weight. He was large and ugly and almost dead.

"What do you need?" he said.

"I'm looking for someone who lives here, an eye doctor?"

He started laughing at me and his grotesquely fat belly shook as it tried to break out of his dirty and torn-up T-shirt.

"What do you think this is, the Tajmit Hall? There ain't no doctors living here, sport." I hated the fat man.

"Well, is there a man about six feet tall, with brown hair, with a lot of dogs, who's been here for a few months?"

"I ain't in the business of finding people, kid. Unless you're interested in renting a space, why don't you go back to the YMCA and screw yourself?"

I was just about ready to let him know that fat people who watch pornos in the front office of trailer parks need some courtesy training, when my dad walked in the door.

"Hey, Charon, do I have any mail?"

He didn't recognize me at first and I barely recognized him. He was a little heavier than I remembered, his hair was long and gray and he had a beard that hung all the way down to the bottom of his neck.

"No mail, not today," Charon said.

"Dad, it's Simeon."

He looked up at me with his big eyes and took a step back. Right then two scrawny mutts trotted into the door and the fat man yelled, "Get out of here. Get. Get out." My dad opened the door and let them out, then continued to walk out the door. I didn't know what to do so I just followed him. I smelled alcohol on his breath.

"Simeon, I can't believe you're here. Sorry you have to find me in this place."

"It's okay, Dad, I'm just glad you came when you did. That guy is a little weird."

"Charon? He's all right. He used to be the head of some Hell's Angels gang. He looks mean but he's a softie." He was fidgeting a lot. "Well, why don't you park by my place? Come on up."

He put his two mutts in his old car and I got in the Volvo and followed him up the dark, dirt road surrounded by broken dreams and spousal abuse. Or, so I thought. I was shaking. I couldn't believe I had found him. He didn't yell at me or insult me or anything. He looked terrible. I looked at my hands and looked at my eyes in the rearview mirror as I was driving and realized I looked a lot like him. My stomach hurt and I realized I should have eaten something before I made it to hell. I followed him to the furthest corner of the park, his trailer was up against a mountain and was gray and brown, but surprisingly well maintained. It was one of the nicer trailers in the park. He got out of his car, the dogs jumped out and started barking at me and he walked over to my car. I didn't know what to do or say next so I just blurted it out.

"Grandma died last weekend, Dad, on my birthday."

He turned from me and walked into his house or whatever you're supposed to call it. He held open the door and turned to me.

"I'm sorry about that, Simeon. Come in and sit down."

I walked into the trailer and couldn't believe my eyes. The whole thing was filled with books. It was like the bookmobile. He had Native American art all over the place and paintings and scrolls and bottles of tequila. There were blankets everywhere, Native American blankets and even a totem pole. I looked at a framed scroll on the wall that read,

> I have pine wind for sale
> have you ever tried it
> three tons of gold
> gets you a gourdful"
> (Lou Tug-pin 8th Century)

"That's great, isn't it? It's kind of my motto nowadays. It was written by one of the eight immortals in China." I was floored by who he was now, almost like a modern-day mystic, living in a trailer park, drunk most of the time, but thoughtful, at least. We sat down in the dark. "How did she die?" he asked while pulling out a bottle of tequila. He poured us each a shot.

"Colon cancer," I said. "I was there visiting Mom for my birthday. She died with her hands in a prayer-like position."

"She always was a faithful woman, even in the end," he said.

We both took our shot. I should have eaten something. Then he poured another round. We took it.

"You came here to tell me that."

I was afraid he was going to get angry.

"Yes, and to see how you were doing."

"Well, how does it look like I'm doing, Simeon?"

I wasn't sure how I was supposed to answer that question.

"Okay, I guess," I said.

He poured another shot for us. That was three in about two minutes. We took it. The lights were still off.

"That's enough tequila for me. Do you want a beer or something?"

"Sure," I said.

I was already feeling it. What was I supposed to do now? I couldn't refuse his medicine. I needed it. I couldn't handle this thing sober, that was for sure. I wouldn't have to worry about that. I was already dizzy. He got up and went to his mini-refrigerator and pulled out two beers.

"Talk to me, son," he said. "It's been a long time."

I could feel tears well up in my eyes. I just wanted to cry and make all of this go away and wake up in a small home in Arizona with River. I mustered up some strength. The tequila helped. I took a sip of beer.

"Well, I'm going to school and still writing for a tractor magazine and that's about it."

"What are you studying?"

"Ancient Greek," I said.

"Really?" he said. "Good for you."

Then he amazed me. He recited part of the first line of the *Odyssey* in Greek. "Andra moi enepe mousa, polutropon …"

"I didn't know you knew Greek," I said.

"There's a lot you don't know about me, Sim, which is my fault, but I don't want to get into that."

I was buzzed. "That's wild," I said. I was getting excited like a boy gets when he sees his dad walk up to the field during a little league game. I was up to bat and sitting in a trailer, half drunk from tequila finding out about my dad. I wanted to go home but curiosity and the love a son has for his father regardless of his actions kept me there. I wasn't in any shape to drive, anyway. I pictured myself trying to maneuver the Volvo and bumping into stray dogs and knocking over trailers and Harleys. I was opening and closing my eyes at a rapid rate.

"You smoke?" my dad asked.

"Yeah, I do." I said.

He handed me a cigarette and lit it for me. This was it, I thought. My dad and I, sitting in his bookmobile getting bombed and smoking cigarettes. No wonder I had trouble with relationships. He turned on a light in the kitchen and I looked at his large frame and his legs and his hands and his hair and wondered if someday I would inherit his trailer and move into the Mountain Trailer Park. The thought made me uncomfortable.

"How long are you staying?" he asked.

"I don't know. I wasn't sure what would happen. I didn't even know if I would find you."

"So, what does that mean?" he asked.

I was afraid he was going to get mad and freak out or something, so I tried to be passive.

"I'm here for the weekend. I don't have to be home until Sunday night." He shook his head and looked like he was planning something in his tequila-filled head.

"Good. I'm glad you're here. I've got a lot to show you." Show me? Here is a man who abandoned me and my mom, was hiding out and had been for years and now wanted to know if I had the time in my busy schedule to spend some time with him.

I said, "Why don't we just see how this goes? It's been a long time, Dad." I looked at him confidently. The tequila helped. I wanted him to know I wasn't a toy he could drink with for a weekend and then go back to his strange ways.

"Okay, Sim. I would like it if you stayed. There's an extra couch you can sleep on."

I just shook my head. I took a sip of beer and a drag of my cigarette. I don't know if it was the alcohol or River or my age or what, but I felt different than I've ever felt. I missed him, even though I didn't like who he was or who I thought he was. A son needs a father. I needed a father and not some fake one like B.D. that

I had to pay for to learn from. I didn't think so before I came here. I was sure that being with my dad would make me feel worse, but, even though we were in a trailer with one light drinking tequila, I was proud. Proud that at least I had a father, and one who wanted me to spend the weekend with him. I wanted to call my mom.

Thoughts swirled in my head as we sat there in the kitchenette drinking our beers and smoking our cigarettes. I was conscious of the fact that I didn't want to be him when I got older, but at the same time I was trying to get rid of that impulse. Maybe if I just took him for what he was and dispelled my thoughts of becoming him I would feel better. I tried that. It didn't work for very long. We were silent. Drinking.

"Do you want to watch TV or something?" he asked.

"No, that's okay," I said. And then it began.

"Good, because I don't have a TV and you shouldn't, either," he said.

Uh oh. He was fidgeting. "Okay," I said, and felt my shoulders melt and my head drop down in a defeated pose. He looked up at me and for the first time I got the chance to look into his deep, blue eyes. They were old, and a little red and fading and had a tint of yellow tequila around the edges. He grabbed us two more beers and then sat back down.

"You must hate me," he said. I started to feel tears entering my eyes. I couldn't stop them. I was in the shadow of the totem pole so he could barely see my face. I tried to stop the tears.

"I don't hate you, I just don't know you." I said. Two tears fell. I sat up and tried to be a man.

"What you know you hate, right?" he said.

"No, not at all." I couldn't stop the tears anymore.

"Well, I don't blame you, Sim," he said kindly. "I hate myself sometimes." Then the storm drain broke. He put his hand on my shoulder and I could feel his huge hands. I wiped my nose and he got up and went to the cupboard and I wiped my tears and tried to collect myself.

Then my life got bizarre. He walked over to me and I thought he was going to hug me or tell me he loved me, but he pulled out a tiny vial from his pocket, put it up to my face and let my tears fall into the tiny opening. What in God's name was he doing? I pulled his hand away and he looked guilty.

"What are you doing?" I asked, still crying.

"I'm collecting your tears."

"Why in the hell are you doing that?" I asked.

"That's what I do."

The room started to spin uncontrollably and I felt like I was going to get sick. I stood up and opened the flimsy door of the trailer, walked outside and vomited. It smelled of tequila, beer and cheap coffee. I was drunk and sick. I threw up again. My back was up against the trailer and I heard the door open and the tear collector walked out with some water.

"That's strong tequila. You're probably not used to it."

203

"I don't think it was the tequila," I said. "Why the hell did you put my tears in a vial?"

He didn't say anything and I fell down to my knees and threw up again. I took a sip of water.

"Why don't you come sit down inside?" he said. He helped me up the mini-stairs and onto the couch and that's all I remember. I passed out, I guess. I was so confused and sick and drunk that my body just shut down and took me away from the old tear collector and gave me some time to rest. I woke up at one point during the night and needed to go to the bathroom, but when I opened my eyes I could see my dad in the kitchenette reading by candlelight and I didn't have any more strength, so I closed my eyes and went back to sleep.

CHAPTER 15

When I woke up he was still in the same chair, asleep, with a book in his hand and the candle burning. I sat up. I didn't feel as bad as I thought I would. Apparently upchucking all that tequila and beer got rid of whatever it is that causes hangovers. I needed some fresh air, so I opened the door and walked outside. The whole park was asleep. I walked around a little and was struck by all the trash and all the dogs and how I had just spent the night in hell and I was still alive. Barely.

My dad was a drunken tear collector. I wasn't sure if he tried to make me cry so he could put my tears in a vial or if it just happened that way. I wanted to call my mom or Peter or River or someone and just disappear. I was stuck in hell, though, with my dad as my only guide. Walking back to the trailer I heard him walking around inside and I got up the courage to go back in. He saw me, even though he was staggering a bit, and said, "Rough night, huh, Sim?"

Rough night? He filled me with tequila, stole my tears and made me sick. He walked over to me with the vial of tears that now had a label on it that read, "Simeon, age 24, a son reappears."

"Don't be overanxious, son," he said. "I'll explain it all to you later. There's a reason for everything. You'll learn that someday."

I didn't have the strength to respond. I know there are reasons for wars and disease and for pain and for money and for cars and for pollution, for God and for babies and other things. I knew that. I didn't, however, make the connection to a non-existent father making me cry and then stealing my tears. I decided to blurt something.

"Whatever you say, Rasputin." I was mad. I stared right at him.

"Do you know anything about Rasputin, Simeon Stylos, or do you just think you're funny?"

We were headed in the wrong direction.

"I know he thought he was God and I'm wondering, as you sit here in this white trash hell, if maybe you think you're divine as well?"

I don't remember ever being that articulate. Especially to an older man who is my father.

"I know I'm not God, and I know a lot about God. Do you?"

Great. We were going to fight about religion as we sat in his trailer.

"I obviously know a different God than you. The God I pray to wouldn't be too proud of a man so immature that he can't call his own son."

I didn't know where all of this was coming from.

"Oh, really, Sim, what God is that?"

He walked over to me and looked like he was going to hit me. I don't remember my dad ever hitting me, but I could tell he had the potential. I took a step back.

"Forget it, Dad," I said, and took a deep breath. I was mad at my mom for urging me to come to this pit. I was mad at Andrew for telling me this was a good idea. He was just out of the loony bin for obsessively launching rockets, why in the heck did I listen to him? My dad sat down.

"I'm sorry, Sim," he said. "Let's get some breakfast and I'll try to explain things to you. Let me do that, and then you're free to go on your way and picture me however you please."

I agreed. I wanted to get in my car and go home and forget I even had a father, but I stayed. As it turns out, I'm glad I did.

He drove me into town in his beat-up car and pulled up next to a bagel shop and walked up to the counter.

"Good morning," the elderly man at the counter said.

"Morning, Ray," my dad replied. "This is my son, Simeon."

The man's eyes lit up. "So, you're the Simeon he always talks about. The writer, right?"

I shook his hand. I couldn't believe my dad ever talked about me, especially not to some man at the bagel shop. "Your dad and I have been friends for some time, Simeon. He fixed my eyes."

I started thinking about all the people who didn't like my dad for not fixing their eyes and for seeing pink elephants. My dad ordered for us and we sat down. Coffee made me feel ten times better and the bagel helped my stomach. I was still feeling a little queasy from the tequila experience. Then my dad spoke. "Ray and I are in a book club together. We're now reading stories about Chinese monks and some poetry."

"That's interesting," I said. He was different this morning. His eyes were clear and he had a kind way about him.

"So tell me what you're studying in Greek, Sim."

"Well," I said, "I'm only in my second year of studying the language, but now we're reading selections from the "Gospel of Matthew and Homer's *Odyssey*.

"I think it's great that you're learning Greek," he said. "Have you tried Latin?"

"Yeah," I said. "I took Latin for two years at Barryman College, but I like Greek better."

"I do, too," he said.

"When did you learn Greek, Dad?" I asked him and the word "Dad" woke us both up. I said it right to him and I guess that means he really is my father.

"I started studying it before medical school and when your mom and I got divorced I traveled for a little while and started studying it more in depth. I was really interested in the Desert Fathers and reading the Gospels in Greek." I couldn't believe what I was hearing.

"Have you read all the Gospels in Greek?"

"No, just Matthew and Mark, those are the only ones I'm interested in."

"Oh." I said.

"Well, what about the Desert Fathers?"

"I've read most of the excerpts from the Desert Fathers and almost all of the *Odyssey* and most of the *Illiad*."

My dad the Classical scholar. I couldn't believe it.

"Why are you so interested in Greek?"

"Your mom didn't tell you much about me, did she?"

"No, just that you left us for a Moroccan woman and you were a good eye doctor and you drank too much."

I couldn't believe I said that. Where did I get the strength?

"Well, that's all true, Simeon, but there's more to me than that," he said.

He proceeded to tell me more about his life. Evidently before he met my mom he had decided he was going to go into the priesthood. He studied with the Jesuits at a seminary in Massachusetts for three years after college. He learned Greek and Latin and German and French and got a classical education. He was interested in overseas missionary work, but when it came time for him to commit to three more years in the seminary and a life of poverty and celibacy, he decided to leave the order. Then he met my mom and decided to become an eye doctor.

"I figured if I couldn't help people find God, I decided I could help them see Him in the world."

I almost fell out of my chair. My heart was jumping up and down. My dad, a man who drinks a quart of tequila a day, lives in a trailer park and is hiding from the Pink Elephant Commission almost

209

became a Jesuit priest? I was at a complete loss. I sincerely didn't understand the man who made me.

He told me that the reason he and my grandma were so close is that when he was a young boy in Richardton she taught catechism classes at the Assumption Abbey. She had him pegged to become a Benedictine monk because of his zeal and his knowledge of scripture. He attended her classes until he was confirmed at age thirteen. She was there that day and, according to him, had always prayed he would become a priest. He kept in contact with her throughout college and seminary, and, when he decided to leave the Jesuits, my grandma set him up with my mom. That's how the story went, according to him. I wished I had asked my grandma more about the story when she was still with us. I couldn't believe what I was hearing. Last night he was an odd, drunk recluse who stole my tears and this morning he was the kind, faithful intellectual renegade I had always wanted to become. I was dizzy. We got up and he said, "Simeon, stay with me for another couple of hours. There's something I want to show you."

"Okay," I said. I wanted to learn more.

We drove back to the trailer park and got out of the car. He had gotten some more bagels from Ray and when we got inside the house he put them and some beer in a backpack, grabbed the vial with my name on it, put it in a toolbox with some other vials and we walked out the door.

"I want to show you where I spend most of my time." Things were getting odd again. I followed him up the trail that led away from the park.

"You know I'm not allowed to practice optometry any more and I haven't done it for almost four years."

"Yeah, I know that," I said as we hiked up a hill with a creek running by it.

"Well, there's a statute of limitations on medical suits of five years, so I've been waiting for that to expire and then I want to get back into practicing."

So that was why he was hiding out. I knew he couldn't practice, but I thought … well, I don't know what I thought, but I was happy to know that he wanted to be a normal working man someday. We continued to hike up the mountains for about twenty minutes until we came upon an abandoned mine.

"This is it," he said.

"What is it?" I asked.

"This is my home away from home," he said. "This is where I spend most of my days."

"Right here?" I asked.

"No, not right here," he said. "In the cave."

If this had happened before I heard all about his life I think I would have run down the hill, barged into the fat man's office, turned down his sex volume, abandoned my car and called Peter to come pick me up in the pink Thunderbird. I didn't want to now, though. We walked into his cave and he lit some candles and I saw books and blankets and paintings and then he lit the candle on his shrine. It was huge and must have housed 200 vials, all like the one that he had used on me.

"This might seem a little weird to you, Simeon, but let me explain."

Weird was not the word. Nothing could seem too weird at this point. He placed my vial in a stack next to the rest of them.

"I collect tears," he said as he cracked open a beer and handed me one. I decided to open it. He took a big sip. He was nervous. He took a deep breath.

"I've never really understood life. I mean the pain of life and the pain I've caused people and the things that have happened to me. The only thing I know, besides the fact that I'm a sinful man, is that tears cleanse people. Tears make people forget, they break you down and then build you up, all at once. So, in my effort to understand people and life, I decided a few years ago to collect tears. There is a vial for every one of my patients that I hurt. The hundred or so who see elephants now are all represented here. Now, there are tears from you. I come up here, almost every day, and look at them and pick up individual vials and pray that I will be forgiven. And now, after you leave, I can come up here and hold your tears in my hands and pray that you'll forgive me for being a terrible father."

I stood there. Something urged me to go towards him. I moved closer and began to feel nervous and sad. He walked towards me and I put my arms around him and hugged him. There we were in his cave, surrounded by the tears of all the people he had hurt in life, and he began to cry. I could feel his chest against mine and his heart beating fast. He stepped away, wiped his tears from his face and took a few steps towards the entrance to his cave. I remained inside for a few moments and looked over all his books and looked at the labels on the vials and felt, surprisingly, calm. He opened another beer.

"I've never shown this to anyone or told them about it. I suppose I never will. This is just where I come to be alone with God and my thoughts. It's the only place I feel comfortable."

We stood there for a moment, drinking our beers, and he picked up a book and handed it to me.

"Read this when you get home, it's about your patron saint, Saint Simeon the Stylite. I read it when I was in the seminary and was so struck by this saint that I wanted to name you after him, so he could guide you in life."

I was amazed. I knew my name was odd and ancient, but I had no idea that I was named after a saint. I felt so much love for my dad at that moment that it's difficult for me to describe. The thought that he named me after someone from whom he had found strength, and the fact that he took so much care in naming me, made me feel, for once, like I was a son.

We walked back down the hill in silence. I kept the book close to my heart as we walked down the hill, making sure nothing happened to it. We got back to the park and I decided I should head back to Santa Barbara. I think he was ready for me to go. I grabbed my things from inside and told him I was going to leave.

"I think it's time for me to go, Dad," I said.

"Yeah, you better get back, Simeon Stylos," he grinned. "Back to the world."

I hugged him again and headed towards my car and he spoke.

213

"You know, I have a subscription to your magazine, I read it every month. You're a good writer. You should think about writing a book someday, when you're ready."

"Thanks, Dad, I hope to." I got in the Volvo and she fired right up. I pulled away from my father, and, as I drove through the rusted-out entrance, I could feel tears well up in my eyes. They were tears of happiness this time, tears of forgiveness and reunion.

CHAPTER 16

I made my way back down the I-5, with my left hand out the window of the princess, smoking cigarettes and flicking them into an old coffee cup on the passenger seat. I breathed a sigh of relief. I was thinking about work and about my last story and about Peter and Dr. Diesel's trip to the Spam Championship in Dallas. They were leaving at the end of the week. I had some ideas on what they should make, but I wasn't sure if they were going to go with the Spamdorf or if they had to come up with another dish. I missed them.

I couldn't wait to tell Peter all about my dad and how strange the weekend was, but how it ended well. I mean, not well if you're a normal person with a normal father, but I'm not. I'm Simeon, son of a modern-day mystic, fueled by tequila and vials of tears, praying for forgiveness in a cave above a trailer park. If that's how you want to look at it, maybe it wasn't the greatest weekend a son can have, but at least I know my dad has feelings. That's all I really wanted to know.

He can love, even if it's projected onto little glass vials and a few dogs. At least the man has potential.

I was the eternal optimist, indefatigable, searching for the good in all men, Chinese restaurants and tractor owners, lover of a river and keeper of an ancient cancer remedy. No wonder Keana was so smitten by me. I can't blame her. I can't blame Elena either, for wanting to leave the tanned jackal for a man of my intellectual and physical traits. I thought again about Odysseus and his weak son, Telemachus, and how their reunion was much more manly and much more desperate, and how when Odysseus returned he inspired his son with courage, hope and honor. How the two of them outsmarted the suitors and the devious staff of his palace and slaughtered them all and took back his kingdom.

We didn't do anything like that, but I did find my father after he had been gone for over twenty years and he did hug me and steal my tears for his shrine. He was eventually going to take back his optometry kingdom, once the elephants couldn't get him any longer. He wasn't going to reunite with my mother, though, which, in the end, was a good thing.

I took my time driving home, which was fine because the Volvo ran best in the slow lane.

I made it back home around dinner time and, after a long, hot shower, checked my messages. One was from Peter checking in on me and the other was from Alan. He sounded sad, so I called him back first. When he picked up the phone I could tell he was depressed.

"How are you, Alan?" I said.

"Not so great, Simeon. I'm a little bored. I used to spend every Saturday night at the gym or at some lecture at B.D.'s house and now, to tell you the truth, I'm not sure what to do with myself." I felt bad for him.

"Well, Alan, I'm kind of bored as well, and I've had a wing-ding of a weekend. Do you want to go out to a movie or something? I bet it would be cheaper than a fifty-dollar lecture from the healer."

He laughed. "That sounds great," he said, relieved.

"I'll find us a movie and call you back," I said.

I called Peter back and left him a message about the weekend without any details and asked him about the Spamdorf and if he thought it had the potential to go the distance. I got ready and picked up Alan and we spent the night out watching a comedy about four sisters and an automotive shop.

On Sunday morning, after about ten cups of coffee, I picked up the book my father had given me. It was a historical account of two Saint Simeons. The first part was about Saint Simeon the Stylite (389-459), my patron saint, and it told of how he left the world and erected a huge pillar and spent the rest of his life on it, without ever coming down. He did it in protest to the world and because he thought society had gone awry and so he could spend his time in prayer and fasting. There were parts in Greek from a man named Theodoret who had known St. Simeon in Syria and seen him perform many miracles and talked with him. I read about his childhood and about how he had heard the Beatitudes at age thirteen and been moved to an extraordinary life.

I then read about St. Simeon Neotheologos, a later Simeon, abbot of Saint Mamas from 980-998, who wrote most of his work in exile near Chrysopolis on the Asiatic shore of the Bosphorus. He wrote about tears being the gift of baptism from the Holy Spirit. It was interesting stuff, with Greek excerpts, which I could now read. I started to understand my dad and why he chose to name me after these men. I wasn't sure how he had interpreted their lives, or how they had influenced him. Maybe they hadn't. Maybe he couldn't live an exemplary life, or even a normal one, and that was why he was so attracted to them. Maybe he wanted to but was too bogged down by tequila and caves and eyes. I don't know but I was beginning to get an idea. I had a great idea. I was filled with the desire to write something, anything, about all of this stuff. Not about tractors and the men who man them, but about real things, this Simeon stuff and about what happened to me at the Pure USA Gym.

My head was filled with ideas. I couldn't wait to tell someone about it, or to start writing. So, that's exactly what I did. I sat down, brewed more coffee, ate three donuts and began to write a play called, appropriately, "A Saint's Last Tear." It would be about me and the St. Simeons, and my dad and life and real things. Maybe I would include some tractors, how could I not? I had never felt so sure about anything in my life. I wrote all day and into the night and never looked back. "A Saint's Last Tear" was becoming a reality.

Monday morning in the office I talked to Peter and Andrew about the weekend and all that had happened.   They listened compassionately. I think it makes a difference who you open up to. I know Peter had been through a few things in his life and I know all about Andrew's struggles, at least some of them, so they were a good audience. They were amazed that my dad was such a recluse and about the cave and the tears and all. Then, with the elation of a man winning his first tractor pull, I told them about my play.

"Well, I'm writing a play, a one-act play, about all of this. I started yesterday and got a large chunk done. It's about us, you guys, my dad, the other Simeons, Pure USA and everything. It's helping me make sense of all of that. And it's good."

"Can I be in it?" Andrew asked.

"Yes, of course you can. And I want Dr. Diesel to be in it and you, Peter, and I'm working out the rest of the cast."

"Are you just writing it, or are you planning on having it performed?" Peter asked.

"Yes, I mean no and yes. I'm writing it, but I want to enter it into the New Playwright contest at the Robber Theater next month. They accept plays from new writers. I have to send it in by the end of this week."

"Great." said Andrew. "I was in a play at the hospital and I must say, I was a big hit." I'm sure he was.

I was filled with so much energy, so much creative strength that I kept a pad of paper with me and all day long I wrote ideas down and dialogue and what the scenes would look like and all. I was happy. I did, however, have to write a story that was due at the end of the day. Peter reminded me of that.

I sat down, took a deep breath and wrote my story. It was another human interest story. Peter liked the way I wrote human interest stories, so he was writing most of the technical stuff himself and having Andrew do the research. My story was about a young veterinarian named Hamburg in, of all places, North Dakota who had turned the farming community upside down with his essay in the "Farming Times" about a new diet designed just for farmers and their families. It was an interesting story. I called around and talked to a few people who had gone on his diet and wrote this story:

Let's face it. The farming community, as a whole, is 40% heavier than normal working folk. It's true. We're a big group. Sitting on top of tractors all day, pushing dirt, making love to the earth, creating life in the form of food, planting hope. It's poetic work, but work that, for some reason, has most of the tractor-driving community thick in the gut and legs. What do we do? Hold on. Don't go haywire on us. The thought of going to a gym, eating ricecakes and cottage cheese like our yuppie counterparts ain't the answer. In fact, I think it's safe to say that if that were the only answer, the only way out, the farming community would just keep eating until we got so big the yuppies would all have to move to Belgium for lack of space. Anyway, here's what Dr. Hamburg said.

"Well, it's real simple. I've been treating cows with this herbal remedy made up of wheat grass and saw palmetto, just as an experiment to see if it made them more lean. I found out that not only did their body fat decrease by at least 30%, but they also seemed happier. So I said, what the hay, I'll try it. It can't hurt. I did and I lost thirty-nine pounds in two weeks and started playing the piano again. My whole family is on it and it's working wonders. So, I figured, it's natural, why not tell the farming community about it?"

And on and on. Peter did like the story and actually ordered some of the Cow Love from Dr. Hamburg for us to try. It was all natural so I figured it couldn't hurt. Peter took out the part about Belgium from the story but printed the rest. We had pictures of cows and Dr. Hamburg's family before and after the Cow Love to run with the story. And that was it. I made it home that night and continued working on the play and decided I would call my mom and tell her about the weekend. I called Hope House and the River answered.

"Hope House, this is Keana."

"Keana, this is Simeon."

"Hi, Sim, how are you?"

"Great. How are you doing?" I said.

"Okay, I'm getting a little sad, though, because I'm leaving in two weeks and I will miss this place."

She went on about how much she had learned from my mom and how she didn't want to leave the kids because she felt like they were too used to abandonment.

"You've helped them all, Keana. They won't forget that."

"Thanks, Sim. I wrote you a letter, did you get it?"

"No, not yet, but thank you," I said.

"Well, your mom is right here, Sim. I'll talk to you soon." Soon. I loved that word. I couldn't wait until that soon came.

I talked to my mom and told her I had found my dad and about how we talked about he and grandma and how he was going to be a priest and all. And I told her how he was going to go back to work

221

when the statute of limitations was over and about all the good things I found out. I left out the tequila part and how he stole my tears and made me sick and the cave. I didn't think she needed to know that. I'm sure she had some idea that he was bizarre; she was married to him for ten years. I could tell she wanted to ask me more questions, like if he was with another woman and things like that, but she didn't. Her voice was more reserved than normal. I decided to cheer her up with the good news.

"Mom, I'm writing a play, about the ancient Simeons and life and Dad and other things. It's called "A Saint's Last Tear" and it's almost done. I mean, I have to finish it this week to get it into an amateur play contest in town."

"That's great, Simeon. Good for you."

"Well, if I get into the contest, will you come out and see it?"

"Of course I will, Simeon. I would be honored. Will I be your date or will you be asking someone else to accompany you?"

"Well, we'll see. I guess Keana wrote me a letter so I might have a date, Mom, but you'll be my distinguished guest."

"That sounds perfect, Simeon. You know, Keana hasn't stopped talking about you since you left."

We talked about how she was doing with my grandma gone and she said she felt peaceful but she could use a trip to California. So, I'd better write a good play so she could come out and see it. I hung up and went straight back to working on the play. I wrote for seven hours straight until I fell asleep at the computer.

When Thursday arrived I had finished "A Saint's Last Tear" and put it in an appropriately addressed envelope and sent it out with a prayer that the committee would give it a chance. I would hear on Monday, so that the three playwrights they chose would have almost a month to rehearse.

I went into the office and Dr. Diesel was there. He had found a place to rent in Santa Barbara so he could be closer to L.A. and all the recording studios, but I think he wanted to be closer to Peter. Peter was smiling all day. We talked about the Spam Championships and decided as a group that they were going to go with the Spamdorf.

"I called the Center for Spam Guidelines and they said that most people make new dishes for the championship but that it was not a requirement."

The judges were different so they would have never tried the Spamdorf. They did, however, have to come up with an appetizer to complement the Spamdorf. We sat around and decided the best thing to do was to ask Chef Chen at the Chinese Kingdom what he thought. Peter told me to call him. I did.

"Chinese Kingdom, can I help you?"

"Hi, this is Simeon at the magazine."

Then the phone dropped.

"Chinese Kingdom, can I help you?" It sounded like the Chef himself.

"Chef Chen, this is Simeon from the magazine."

"Ah, Shimeon. You talking to the handsome cowboy."

223

It was the Chef. I told him about our dilemma and after about three minutes of describing the contest and Spam to him, he offered out his suggestion: "Spam Won Tons with lobster sauce." Then he hung up.

I was thinking about their phone manners at the Kingdom and I guess they lose ten to fifteen phone orders a day when they pass the phone around like a hot potato. But we had gotten the suggestion and Dr. Diesel and Peter decided to go there and learn how to make the Won Tons quickly. I, against all logic, asked Peter if I could go home and get some rest. I had been staying up writing all week so I was exhausted. He let me go and he and Rando and Andrew went to the Kingdom. I found out later that Andrew sneaked in a photo of the Chef with the hair dryer and handed it to him and asked him to autograph it, "The handsome cowboy." He did and Andrew put it up by his new desk. He was a clever one.

When I got home I went straight to the mailbox and found Keana's letter sitting with two cancellation notices for my membership to Pure USA. I threw them away and opened the letter.

Dear Simeon, I'm so sorry about your grandma. I feel honored to have gotten to know her over the past three months. She told me so many stories about her childhood and about your mom and you that I feel like I've known your family for years. I'm sure you'll miss her. I know I will.

I really enjoyed spending time with you this past weekend. I hope, when I come home, we can stay in touch and maybe you can come out and see me in Arizona and meet my family. I will miss your mom and every day I spend with her I feel lucky. Write me back. I miss you. Keana.

I read the letter three or four times and then wrote her back and told her about the play and that if I win maybe she could come out and see it and we could spend the weekend together. Nights of love and theater. Life was beginning to get significantly better.

On Friday I went in early and Peter and Rando were in the office for a few hours figuring out the recipes and I tasted the "Spamtons" as they called them and they were excellent. They caught a flight that afternoon with three carry-ons of Spamdorf and Spamton ingredients sitting in ice. Andrew went with them. He was in charge of the refrigeration.

I spent most of the day cleaning out my desk and thinking about the play. I was hoping to hear over the weekend but that was pretty soon. I went home that night and went to bed early with the copy of the book my father had given me on my chest.

I hadn't done any laundry or shopped or eaten correctly all week, so I spent Saturday in an organizational frenzy, and then around dinner time I got the call.

"Sim. It's Peter."

"Peter, did you win?"

"No. We got beat pretty badly."

"What happened?" I asked.

"Well, Chef Chen's recipe won third place and the Spamdorf didn't even make it into the final round."

"Oh, that's too bad, Peter."

"Yeah, but we got a year's supply of Spam, just for being in the Championship round."

We talked for a little bit. He was sad, but not that sad, considering he was in a Spam recipe contest.

"I'll see you on Monday, Sim. Andrew and Rando and I are going to a rodeo tonight, so that should cheer us up."

I thought about Andrew and the rodeo and I wondered if he had gotten a wallet-sized photo of Chef Chen and if, at some point during the rodeo, he was going to pull it out and show it to Peter.

Monday arrived and the rodeo crew returned. I was waiting anxiously for the call from the Robber. It didn't come in the morning. Noon came. Then three o'clock, then four-thirty and then it came.

"Man Tractors, this is Simeon."

"Simeon Stylos?"

"Yes, can I help you?"

"Simeon, this is Rita Litten from the Robber."

"Yes. Hi Rita, how are you?"

"Good, Simeon. I'm calling you to tell you that your play, 'A Saint's Last Tear,' has been chosen by our panel to be featured in our New Playwrights showcase at the end of the month. Congratulations."

"Thank you," I said. "Thank you so much."

"Thank you, Simeon. You're a very talented young man. We look forward to seeing your play. If you can come down here tomorrow we can go over the specifics."

"Thank you. Thanks, again," I said.

I hung up the phone and had tears in my eyes. I looked around the room and Peter was getting something out of his desk and Andrew was walking over to me. The whole thing was in slow motion. I was so happy. The last few months passed before my eyes and then I woke up to the sound of a bottle of champagne opening, and Peter smiling.

"I had a feeling you were going to be chosen," he said. He was my best friend. We all drank a toast to "A Saint's Last Tear," even young Andrew, and Peter called Dr. Diesel and told him the good news.

"Tell him he's in the play," I said. "He's the narrator, I need him."

He told Rando and I immediately called my mom and told her and Keana and asked her to be my date and she said she would drive from Arizona for the event. I had a date for the opening night. I drove down to the Chinese Kingdom after work and walked up to Chef Chen standing under the famous photo by the showers that read, "The staff of the Chinese Kingdom, May we bring you food for lovers and honey chocolate." It was better, but still off.

I told Chef Chen about the play and about how I wanted him to be in it and he took a few steps back and smiled.

"You want handsome cowboy in play?"

"Yes, Chef Chen, I wrote a part for you."

"I have cowboy hat for the show."

I smiled. He was in. The play was on.

CHAPTER 17

We spent the next few weeks going over our parts, practicing in the office and sometimes at the Chinese Kingdom after hours. Andrew was doing great, Dr. Diesel was good and Chef Chen was a born star. The show came upon us so quickly. Dr. Diesel had come up with all the costumes and Peter built the set. My mom flew in on the morning before the big night and she met Keana for lunch and they spent the day together while we were at the theater putting the final touches on the performance.

I was at the theater most of the day, trying to talk down Andrew who had at this inopportune time, decided being the star might be too much.

"Andrew, you can do it. I need you," I said.

"I know, I know, it's just too much. What if I screw up?"

"You won't," I said. "Your mom is going to be here, Peter is going to be here. You're going to do great."

He smiled, took a deep breath and decided he was going to make it as the main character in my first play.

Five o'clock came. The theater was filling in. I kept looking from behind the curtains to see who was going to show up. We were all assembled and would be the third play to go on. Chef Chen had his cowboy hat on backstage and was walking around in Rando's sequined cowboy boots which were three sizes too big. Andrew had on a monk's outfit and sandals, Rando was wearing the same outfit as well, but it was green. Green was the color of hope.

We waited backstage for the two other plays to finish. The first one was about a rabbit who decided that living in a cage wasn't the life for him so he escaped to the French Riviera and lived in the basement of a ritzy hotel. The next play was about a Martian who came down from Mars and ended up becoming a star in the Ice Capades. They were both good. I had seen them during the dress rehearsal. Then the curtains closed, and it was time for us to go. It was showtime. Andrew was breathing heavily.

"What if I have a panic attack?" he whispered.

"You won't," I said. "I'll be right here, so look over at me if you need strength."

Rita introduced me. I was shaking but proud. I went out to the front of the stage, in all the lights with all the people. The place was packed. I walked up under the lights and spoke.

"My name is Simeon Stylos. I would like to present to you my play, *"A Saint's Last Tear."* People clapped. I started to turn around and noticed a man standing in the back, a man with gray hair and a long beard. It was my dad. He waved at me and smiled. I couldn't believe it. He was here. I walked backstage and the show began.

Andrew and Chef Chen were the first to go out. They looked nervous. Dr. Diesel began the narration from the side of the stage. The lights were on him. He was rapping. Chef Chen was beating a large drum, giving Rando the beat.

The lights came up on Andrew standing on top of the scoop of a tractor, ten feet in the air. He looked like an angel. The lights hit him perfectly, casting a shadow behind the platform. Rando moved to his side. Everything was going perfectly. I was watching from the side of the stage.

Chef Chen was beating the drum. Peter walked out dressed as a beggar. They said their lines like pros. They spoke of diseases in town and of plagues and fears. They were asking the Saint what to do. He told them stories of hope and forgiveness and how he had left the world to live on this tractor and he had been there for over twenty years. Chef Chen stopped beating his drum to say his lines.

"I come from Asia. I heard about a man who had left the world now living on a structure. They said he could perform miracles and give blessings. I've been looking for you for one year." He blurted out the last part.

He began to beat the drum again. Rando was rapping the narration. Andrew spoke to Chef Chen.

"I came here as a boy, but now I'm a man. You can see from the wrinkles on my face and the gray in my hair that nature has aged me. Take this letter I have written and it will help you in your struggles."

They continued. I could hear some laughter and some noise coming from the crowd. They were doing great. Andrew was a star. I looked out behind the curtain and could see my dad standing there, listening to the lines and smiling. I also could see my mom sitting with Keana, both dressed up like they were at the Oscars, and I could see the entire staff of the Chinese Kingdom dressed for work, sitting together waving at Chef Chen. They had left a sign on the door of the restaurant that read, "Not closed, not open, come back later after play." We were all going there later for a post-production party.

I listened to my friends project my words to a theater filled with the people I loved and people I would learn to love. Things were in slow motion again. I was watching Andrew stand on the tractor. He was old now, dying, but still giving blessings and advice. Three men, all from different parts of the world, seeking the advice of the Saint, who left the world as a young boy and now, when it was his time to die, would remain standing on his structure in a prayerful pose, a tear running down his cheek.

As I watched Andrew The Letter Writer close his eyes, I began thinking about this past year. I thought about how I had left the world, temporarily with the Pure USA Gym, about how Andrew's letters left the world in his large rockets, and about how my dad had left the world, hiding in a cave above a trailer park. That is what Saint Simeon Stylos did many years ago. He left the world, built a huge column and lived his whole life above the people, but closer to God.

Chef Chen opened the letter the Saint had dropped to him.

"It's in Greek," he said.

"What does it say?" asked Dr. Diesel.

Chef Chen continued, "Without purity of soul he will never attain purity of body. Without water it is impossible to wash a dirty garment clean, and without tears it is even more impossible to wash and cleanse the soul from pollution and stains."

Chef Chen paused. "There's more," he said.

"Blessed are the ones who mourn or grieve, for they will be comforted.

Blessed are the peace makers, for they will be named sons of God.

Blessed are those showing mercy, for they will receive mercy."

And the lights went out and the curtains closed on my play. I stood in front of my friends and smiled. It was over. I heard clapping. I looked out from behind the curtain and I could see tears in the eyes of people I loved. Good tears. Tears of hope and forgiveness. And then, of course, my tears came.

The End